MENTAL TC 10

Interviews with 7 of the World's Greatest
Professional Tennis Coaches

On what it takes to be
a mentally tough tennis player…
& person.

By: Greg LeVine

With interviews from:

Michael Center

Philip Farmer

Ellis Ferreira

Luke Jensen

Chuck Kriese

Bruce Levine

Jeff Wilson

*Thank you for your interest in "Mental Toughness 101"!
I hope you learn, grow and become mentally tougher
because of it!*

Thank you and all the best,

-Greg

greglevine@bellsouth.net
www.facebook.com/mentallytoughnow

CONTENTS

INTRODUCTION: 4
"Why I wrote a book on mental toughness."

INTERVIEW #1: Michael Center 9
Head Coach of the University of Texas Men's Tennis team

INTERVIEW #2: Philip Farmer 29
Coach of top 20 world touring professional tennis players
and the #1 doubles team in the world

INTERVIEW #3: Ellis Ferreira 51
Former #1 doubles player in the world

INTERVIEW #4: Luke Jensen 67
1993 French Open Doubles Champion with brother Murphy
Jensen; ESPN Tennis Analyst since 1994; Syracuse University
Head Women's Tennis Coach 2006-2014

INTERVIEW #5: Chuck Kriese 91
Hall of Fame Coach, Author of four books on tennis; Coach of
five Grand Slam Junior titles

INTERVIEW #6: Bruce Levine 117
Former professional tennis player and coach of both professional
men and women tennis players

INTERVIEW #7: Jeff Wilson 141
CEO and co-owner of the MW Tennis Academy at the Family
Circle Tennis Center; Coached six Top 100 Women's
Tennis players

Introduction:

"Why I wrote a book on mental toughness"

Since I was five years old, I've been playing the game of tennis. I've always loved the intensity of competition and the joy of winning. The satisfaction that comes from achieving a seemingly unattainable goal through hard work and perseverance is one of the great experiences of life. However, I often found, to my frustration, that my ambition to win at sports—specifically tennis—would often get in the way of my performance. I found myself playing at a lower and safe level, just to obtain the coveted "victory." Subsequently, it's through the challenge to bring forth my best effort every time I step out onto the court that I came to understand the value and importance of the mental aspect of tennis.

Therefore, after graduating with a degree in Psychology, I enrolled in a Personal/Life/Business coaching program in the hopes of creating a mental toughness program for athletes. This program, now in existence, has improved the games of many athletes by helping them understand what it takes to have the mentality of a champion. I use the combination of Psychology and Personal Coaching to help athletes eliminate self-defeating habits, develop their self-confidence, and transform negative attitudes and behaviors.

Then two years ago, I attended a conference about the importance of writing a book to take your business's mission to the next level. With this motivation, I recognized a great opportunity: to create a book based on the interviews of world-renowned professional tennis coaches and former professional tennis players. By interviewing top professionals who have played and coached at the highest levels, I knew I'd gain a tremendous understanding of the importance and value of the mental side of the sport.

I was blessed to be good friends with the "one and only" Patricia Jensen, who was kind enough to share her Rolodex with me and introduce me to some of the most inspiring and insightful tennis personalities around. It was through these introductions and interviews that this project was born.

Within the pages of this book, you'll hear from the following distinguished mentors of the game of tennis:

- **Michael Center:** Head Coach of the University of Texas

- **Philip Farmer:** Coach of top 20 world touring professional tennis players and the #1 doubles team in the world

- **Ellis Ferreira:** Former number-one doubles player in the world

- **Luke Jensen:** 1993 French Open Doubles Champion with brother Murphy Jensen, ESPN Tennis Analyst since 1994, Syracuse University Head Women's Tennis Coach 2006-2014

- **Chuck Kreise:** Hall of Fame coach, author of four books on tennis, coach of five Grand Slam Junior titles

- **Bruce Levine:** Former touring tennis professional and coach of both professional men and women tennis players

- **Jeff Wilson:** CEO and co-owner of the MW Tennis Academy at the Family Circle Tennis Center, Coached six top 100 Women's Tennis players

Each of these interviews is powerful and dynamic in its own way. You, as the reader, will acquire insight into the tools used by these coaches to create a winner's mind and attitude. These are tools that you can apply not only to your tennis game but to whatever endeavor you pursue. Furthermore, the words of these great coaches teach the value of bringing your best effort to anything you pursue, because doing your best is the source of true satisfaction.

.

Michael Center:

Head Coach of the University of Texas
Men's Tennis team

Michael Center

*Head Coach of the University
of Texas Men's Tennis team*

I'll start by asking if you recommend certain pre-match rituals to help players get their heads in the right mind space before a match.

I think rituals are a tricky question. There are certain things that I think you have to do while you're on the court, that you have to practice day in and day out and then take onto the court. Learning how to breathe, having the same routine when you serve—doing the same things over and over again. Mentally, I encourage our guys to picture where they want to serve the ball.

As far as getting warmed up or getting yourself ready to play, I think everyone is different. For example, some players like to warm up a little longer than others. So I don't think that necessarily right before the match everybody has to do the same thing, but I do think there are things that you have to practice leading up to the match on the court so that when you get into the match you're confident, you're ready and you know what you want to do when you're serving the ball—whether it's the first ball in the match or it's 5-all in the third.

So basically, before the match, everybody should create their own unique pre-match ritual?

I think so, yes. With some of our players we typically get

to the court an hour and 15 minutes or so before the match and we stretch, we put on our ankle braces and then we warm up. For doubles we have a little routine we do before we play, but some of the guys like to hit a little bit more than others and some are more ready to go. So I don't like to put them in a box where everybody has to be the same way in their pre-match warm-up.

After players have lost a tough point, how do you recommend they get their minds back in focus?

I think part of playing tennis is learning how to play one point at a time. It's a very simple thing but you've got to use the time in between the point, walk away and make sure your routines come into play. Breathing techniques are useful, and some players like to play with their strings a little bit and then get themselves ready to compete for the next point.

"I think when you can compartmentalize the ability to compete for one shot at a time and not allow something negative to create another negative reaction, that's when you become very mentally focused and tough to beat on the court."

I think when you can compartmentalize the ability to compete for one shot at a time and not allow something negative to create another negative reaction, that's when you become very mentally focused and tough to beat on the court.

How do you avoid bringing that negative emotion from one point to the next?

First off, we talk a lot about our body language. You need to create a positive image out there. We talk about using body language in trying to create the image of "Okay, that's over, I'm ready to go, I'm ready to fight you for the next point." So, I think it starts with your image and how you present it to your opponent.

It's a one-on-one battle and you have to say to yourself, "I might have lost that point and who knows how or why—whether the other guy hit a great shot or got a little lucky or I hit a poor shot—but you know what, that's over. I've now re-grouped and now you can look at me and you can see that I'm mentally and physically very strong." Even though you might be a little shaken up about it, if you practice this technique and you show a lot of positive imagery to your opponent, it reinforces your ability to be ready to start and compete for the next point effectively.

Does it make a difference even if it's match point?

I think as far as showing a positive image, it has to be consistent throughout the match. Sometimes I'll talk to our players and say, "If it gets down to the last point, let's raise our body language even more." I tell them, "Let's show that we're ready to go at it," because one of the mistakes people make is trying to stay so calm under pressure that their energy level comes down.

You have to have a good energy level to be quick and alert to the ball. You don't see a sprinter line up to run a 100-yard dash in a casual stance. They're alert, they're ready, they're energized, and I think the same is true for a tennis player. You've got be alert and active, and if you do that consistently through the match without wasting a lot of energy, you will be in a good emotional and mental state. You don't need to be going crazy, you just need to be creating a lot of positive feeling out there and then you will be ready to win those big points.

How do you get your players to stay strong and focused throughout a long point? What's the trick?

We practice a lot for those situations. I think what you do on the practice court translates into those match-type situations. We might start a point where you have to hit six, eight, 10 balls just cross court before the point even starts. We'll simulate different situations and push our guys. When I get a feel for what their limit is, I'll try to simulate situations that will create practice situations that will put them in long-point situations.

Obviously you're working on their fitness as well so that they feel that they can stay out there, because fatigue will make a coward of us all. If you feel physically strong, then for the most part mentally you can stay strong during those points. But I think that mental edge starts on the practice court in trying to create situations where the player has to work really, really hard just to even start the point and then they have to grind it out.

How do junior tennis players increase their confidence in themselves?

We try to create practice situations where one of the things we don't allow our players to do is have any negative reaction to something that goes wrong. Some of the kids will get down; they'll shake their heads a lot or kick their racquet. We have one guy who likes to punch the fence and we try to reinforce that whether it's through running or through conversation, you cannot allow your emotions to bring you down. Hopefully through this they start to develop confidence.

Tennis is a game of mistakes and people are going to make mistakes and when they do they start to learn, "You know what, that's just one mistake, I'll be ready to compete for the next one." Then they start to build a little more confidence that they can be successful the next time because no one is going to play a perfect tennis match. Anyone who has watched tennis knows that when you watch someone and they make an error—whether it's Federer, Nadal or a club player—how they react to a mistake is a good sign of how they're going to handle tough situations.

So it's tough to say. Some kids have more confidence than others. We try to train them the best we can to keep their mistakes from bringing them down, and that's not an easy thing to do.

Can it ever be positive to let out emotions, so a player shakes it out of himself?

Sometimes a guy will miss a shot and we're not robots, it's not like they're not going to show any emotion or just be perfect all the time. Sometimes I'll let them yell it out a little. By then it's like, "Hey, c'mon now, you have to let that go and you've got to move on to the next point."

If I start to feel like it's trending [into a pattern] or it's hurting their play, that's where the coach comes in and draws the line on that behavior. This is where you've got to have a good feel because everyone is a little bit different. Obviously, if a guy starts smashing racquets then that's crossing the line.

So, a little yell is okay?

Yeah, sure.

What do you recommend players should be doing during a changeover?

First of all, I think you've got to breathe. You've got to really breathe and you've got to try to relax and you've got to start focusing on how you want to be playing after the change-over. You should ask yourself "Okay, where do I want to hit this serve? What serve is working best for me?" or "What do I want to do with the first point? How do I want to tackle this first point?" You need to be thinking during the changeover so when you get up off that bench you have a game plan for what you want to do with that first point.

But I think the main thing there is not to allow your mind to get away from you and be racing with a lot of thoughts. So keep it simple, keep breathing, try to relax your body and have in mind what you want to do when you get up from the bench.

What about when a line judge makes a bad call and a player gets flustered? How do you deal with this type of situation in the most productive way?

There are so many things that happen in tennis—and in life—that are out of your control and that's just one of those things. We face it all the time. I thought we got a pretty tough call in a really tough situation the other night. At that point, I told the players, "You don't argue with the umpire—let me talk to the umpire." So the players are not allowed to argue with the umpire.

If you don't have a coach there, you have to show that you're willing to stand up and say, "Are you sure?" But once the decision is made, it's made! Any energy or time you are using to argue, you are wasting, and potentially creating an adverse effect to get another bad call in the future. I think it's best to have the reputation that you can absorb situations that don't go your way because, as we all know, in life whether it's a line call or other things, if you don't have control over it, there isn't much you can do.

But does that really solve the issue? Typically are your players able to shrug it off with that approach?

I think it depends on their mental toughness and how strong they are and if they've been continuing to try and work on it. If I have a player and I know a bad line call is going to set him off, then that's probably the guy who needs to work at getting mentally stronger. That's something we need to talk about, we need to work on and we will set some parameters. That type of player does not get near the official because if his opponent sees that one call is going to shake him up, then that's going to give the opponent a lot of confidence. And the opponent will be thinking, "Wow, if that one call is going to do it, then there are a lot of other things that can do it."

Once again, we're going back to that perception of good energy, good positive body language and a good attitude, which you always have to demonstrate while you're out on the court. If you can't handle that, then you had better address it and you better figure it out quickly. A good technique is for the player to tell himself, "Number one, I didn't have control over that, and number two, arguing and going nuts is certainly not going to help." I haven't seen very many people argue and go nuts and have that benefit their play. Maybe John McEnroe is the only one.

I guess it's helpful having a conversation about it just to make the player aware of what he looks like, what he's doing, and then hopefully that conversation will help him transform his behavior.

At the end of the day you have to have players who are willing to be coached and who are willing to make adjustments.

With the guys who just want to argue all the time and think they have all the answers, there's not much you can do. You have to have an athlete who's willing to say, "Okay, coach, if you think that's best and you don't think that's helping me, than I am willing to try to get better."

Nerves have the ability to be a positive force for success if channeled correctly. How do you teach your players to channel their butterflies successfully?

Everybody's going to get nervous, and anyone that tells you otherwise is lying. The first thing I tell my players is, "Just accept that you're going to be nervous!" Players need to channel that energy and look at it as a positive, not as a negative, to raise their energy level, because the biggest thing that people typically do when they get really nervous is slow down. Their footwork slows down, their hands slow down and they will push at the ball a little bit.

So I'll talk with the players about raising their energy level, raising their footwork, being real positive and using that nervousness to go after the ball and accelerate through the shots and be aggressive.

Let's say that it is right before a big point and the player is feeling that nervous energy. Do you recommend they jump up and down or run in place?

Yes, jumping up and down before the return is a good method for releasing that energy. Or another option is to hop up and down a little before you walk up to that line and serve. Try to transform those jitters into something that's creating some aggressiveness, because I like players who want to be aggressive in a pressure situation. I think it's too hard to win at this game running around trying to put balls back in play.

What you need is to just be more aggressive because the tendency is just to get passive and tight and push at the ball.

It is tough, though, because when you try to change it you can over exaggerate it too.

Yes, you can over exaggerate, and you don't want to go for the line and try to hit an outright winner the first shot. But I'm just trying to keep them balanced when they're a little nervous, because the biggest problem is that things slow down, particularly their feet. So I want to try to keep their feet moving. In this situation, a player or coach should be saying, "Hey, c'mon, get your feet moving... Bounce around . . . C'mon, let's be aggressive with your feet and hit for big targets."

In your opinion, what's the difference between the professional player who remains around 100 in the world for most of his career and the players who remain in the top 20 for most of their careers?

Typically the top guys have a different talent level. In addition, you've got a combination of everything with Federer and Nadal, who are amazing athletes, incredible workers and mentally as tough as they come. However, when you take those top guys out, the difference between a player who is ranked 20 to 30-something and the player who is ranked 100 is a very small margin.

All the different factors that bring pressure on a player start to separate players and weed out those who are less competitive. The best players are the ones who physically and mentally withstand that pressure the best.

Everybody can play well for a week or a match or stretches in matches, but the player who can absorb it all and grind it out week after week and not get down but stay steady and consistent and grind through matches again and again is going to come out on top. One week these guys are getting ready to play on clay and then they have to turn around and play on grass, then hard court, with significant changes in weather. There are a lot of factors that go into being a successful professional tennis player.

It's not easy—tennis is a tough sport.

Can you give some advice for a junior player who dreams of being a professional tennis player but isn't sure they have the ability? What would you say to them to boost their confidence?

I would tell them, "You can have a long-term goal, but you have to focus on short-term goals right now." I hear a lot of kids say, "I want to be a pro." And my response is, *"Let's be the best that you can be right now. If you're a state-ranked player, or a sectional player, let's keep trying to climb the ladder and go one step at a time. And, when you become good enough to be a professional tennis player, it will become obvious."*

I don't know John Isner that well but I think John Isner went to college trying to be a really good college player and he started to develop and he started to realize, "You know what? I can become a pro."

But if you're always setting that bar, "I have to be a pro," and you don't want to grind through the stages that it takes to become a pro, then I think you put pressure on yourself, you get disappointed more easily, and the game becomes very frustrating. I think if you just kind of take one step at a time and climb that ladder and keep trying to become the best player that you can become at each and every level, you'll find out whether you can become a pro or not.

That's advice for everything—

Exactly: "Let's be the best that you can be today, and if you do the best that you can do each and every day, that's all you can do. That's all you have control over." But I still hear these kids all the time, "I want to be a pro, I want to be a pro," and I'm thinking, You're like 12,15 in your section. There's a long way to go to being a pro. Let's work today on trying to be better. If you do that, one day you'll see if you can be a pro.

It's so easy but it's actually pretty profound.

Yeah, it's easy—but difficult to do.

To become a pro, you've got to enjoy practice. What's your secret for junior players especially to excel at and enjoy practice?

To be good at anything, I tell them, "First of all, you have to love to practice. If you go to practice and it's torturous, then you're not going to become a good tennis player. So you have to love to hit the ball and you have to love to play the game. And it's the first thing you have to realize about yourself. And it's hard work."

Players can do different drills, and we try to end our practices with these doubles drills that are kind of fun and exciting, but the bottom line is that they've got to hit a lot of serves and they're going to have to hit a lot of serves into one spot to master the ability to hit that spot they really need to hit. They're going to have to work on their approach shot or volley, and it just takes a lot of repetition.

I don't think players need to practice four hours at a time, but when we do practice we typically go two hours to two and a half hours. It needs to be pretty focused and the players have to come to the court with an idea of what they want to work on that day. I have a practice plan every day for our team but within that plan one guy may need to work on a specific area and he needs to try to come to the court and get that done.

If a player can come to the court with the mindset, "I'm trying to improve in this area or this is what I'm working on," I think he can use his time well and get a lot better versus "I'm just going to hit balls today." That really doesn't make a player better. He's got to come out there with, "I want to improve my chip backhand today and when I'm doing this drill I'm going to really work on that." And then he's got to really enjoy hitting his chip backhand. That has got to give him pleasure in trying to improve that area of his game.

And you go in there with a plan too.

I go in there with a plan, yes.

How do you recommend young players keep a balanced life but still have the appropriate emphasis on tennis to keep their professional dreams alive?

I'm not a fan of dropping everything and just becoming a tennis player at the age of 10 or 12. I think youngsters should keep playing other sports, doing other things, keep making themselves better athletes and keep trying to live a normal life.

I like to see kids stay at home as much as they can. Go to school, but you might have to get up a little bit earlier and you might have to stay a little bit later sometimes. Try to keep your life in as normal surroundings as possible. I think these kids who go away to academies at the age of 10 or 12 and live away from home and home school right away—I think that's a treacherous trail to go down. It can lead to burnout quickly.

At what point should a junior player take that next step toward a life more committed to tennis?

As you get into your teenage years and you are playing more and more tennis, you might have to give up some of your other sports and spend a little more time on the court. At this point, tennis is going to start to require a certain amount of travel for a junior player to become a good tennis player. You can't play only in your neighborhood, you have to go out and find the competition.

You should try to keep your lifestyle as consistent as possible. You have to learn how to win at the junior level because at the professional level you have to learn how to lose because you're not going to win very many tournaments. You can go the whole year without winning a tournament. You're going to have to be a great player. I don't know what the ranking is of guys who have above 500 records but you probably have to be a top 30, 40 player in the world just to have a 500 or better record on tour.

So there's no rush. You just have to keep grinding it out and keep things as normal as possible and keep up the consistency. If it becomes their whole life at too early an age, I think it becomes too much for the kids and too much for the families. So enjoy the ride, enjoy the game and don't make it bigger than it is when you're 12 years old and you're trying to develop.

Do you use any specific goal-setting practices with your players?

For our players at the University of Texas we have the team write a mission statement at the beginning of each year on what they want to accomplish. After we write the team statement, I bring all the players in individually and ask them to write down the goals that they individually want to accomplish.

I really work hard to emphasize the day-to-day type goals, and have everyone think, *What am I doing today to get myself better?* I think when you create too many expectations and use goal-setting incorrectly, you can end up feeling that if you don't accomplish a certain goal, you're a failure. I think that puts a lot of pressure on the players.

We focus on, "Every year we want to be the conference champions" or "We want to win the national championship." However, we really should be focusing more on "Our first-serve percentage is 60 percent; we want to get that up to 65 percent. What do we need to do to get our first-serve percentage up?" Then we should come to the court every day trying to improve that. By focusing on just what they can improve, the players start to feel like they can be successful and that they're making themselves better. That way they're not focused on too many long-range, high-expectation goals that often will create feelings of failure.

You mentioned that each player writes their own individual goals for the year, correct?

Yes, they write it out at the beginning of the year and then I keep it in their file and then sometimes I'll bring it out and kind of say, "Hey, remember, this is what we're trying to work on—this is what we're trying to do."

As far as the mission statement for the team, they write it together and then we put it up in our locker room.

Then on a weekly basis it's just a personal thing: "Okay, today I'm working on improving my serve"?

Correct. Usually at the end of the semester I'll bring each player in and together we'll look at what goals they wrote down at the beginning of the semester and say, "Okay, these are the things we talked about and here is where we're at. What do we need to do to get better?" I'm a big believer in the day-to-day. "Let's focus on what we're trying to improve today and not get ahead of ourselves."

How do you push your players in those moments when they don't feel like putting in the necessary effort?

If once in a blue moon a player gets burned out and is really just tired or worn out, I might give him the day off. I always try to look for guys who love to play the game. That's one of the things I've learned through the years. I'm looking for guys who just like to hit that tennis ball because I always tell them, "You're going to be as good as what you do when I'm not watching you." If I have to stand on top of a player and say, "C'mon now, hit that forehand" versus I leave practice and I walk back out there later and there's a player with a bucket of balls hitting serves, that's the kind of guy I'm looking for. That's the kind of guy who will usually be more successful.

But if someone's really worn out and he's a good practice player and just needs a day off, then I'll give him a day off. But if he needs a lot of days off and he doesn't like to play, then that's going to be a problem.

Who do you see as the most mentally tough professional players right now on the tour? One man and one woman.

I think you have to go the very top. With Djokovic and Nadal, I'd have to give them a toss-up on who is the toughest. Djokovic has been beating Nadal, but those two guys are just relentless out there. I don't know how you can get any mentally tougher than them. On the women's side, it's hard to say. When Serena is at her best, I don't think you can get more competitive than she is.

What life skills should the serious tennis player hope to gain and take away from living a tennis-focused life?

I think the skill set tennis gives you includes a tremendous amount of discipline.

There are just certain things you have to do every day to be a great tennis player that require a lot of discipline, from getting enough sleep to eating well to taking care of your body to stretching to weight training to fitness to the practice itself. And if you become a really good tennis player, I think you're going to create a lot of discipline in your life and I think it's going to lead to a lot of success. Because the thing about tennis is that you have to work for everything you get. You're not signing a contract out of college and getting paid. Regardless, you've got to earn everything that you get. And you have to keep winning and you have to learn to take care of yourself. The other thing is; you have to be prepared. I've never met a good tennis player who wasn't a really prepared tennis player. And if you can learn those things, you're going to be pretty good and successful in a lot of things at life.

Who is your role model in tennis?

I've had some really good friends who have influenced me. My college coach, Coach Scott Perelman was a big influence on me as a person and as a tennis player. And I always looked up to Dick Gould. I was a volunteer assistant with Coach Gould for two years at Stanford and watched how he motivated and dealt with a lot of great players. There have been a lot of terrific players who have influenced me or affected me along the way, but I had the opportunity to work closely with Coach Perelman and Coach Gould.

Two other coaches that I watched and learned a tremendous amount from were Tut Bartzen, who was an excellent coach at TCU [Texas Christian University], and Dave Snyder, who I replaced here at Texas. They significantly influenced me. The main things I learned from them were their ability to motivate their players and their understanding of how to be good managers of people.

What does it take to be a good motivator?

A good motivator is a good communicator who must be able to communicate effectively with different types of people. A good motivator has to be able to recognize that people are different and has to try to dig into different people in different ways to understand them. Additionally, a good motivator must be willing to adjust to different situations. I think that's why certain coaches become great, because they can withstand time and the ability to communicate and motivate different types of people.

In closing, I'd just like to say that it really comes down to one thing. Do you want to play well or compete to your fullest. If you choose to compete you will find out how good you can be. If not your results will bounce around like a rubber ball.

2

Philip Farmer:

Coach of top 20 world touring
professional tennis players and the
#1 doubles team in the world

Philip Farmer

Coach of top 20 world touring
professional tennis players and the
#1 doubles team in the world

What pre-match rituals do you recommend for players to get their heads into the right space before a match?

I think it's good to always have written scripts. I'm a big believer in positive thinking, and going over different scripts is great for that. The script is unique to each player. A player might use a script containing positive affirmations such as, "I have a great serve," "I'm going to play aggressively," or "I'm going to play to win." Another script might talk about relaxation: "I'm going to stay calm and stay balanced." A script might be about strategy or the game plan. It's good to get into a routine where you have scripts to read. The script can be in a notebook or on a laminated sheet of paper, and you go over it before your match. It gets you into the right state of mind to go out there with a game plan.

We all have plans, obviously, relating to our game and our style of play, but a lot of the time we don't go out there with our game plan in our mind. You want to go out there and be relaxed, be very positive, and be really committed to your own system of how you want to play and what you want to do during the match.

How long is a script, typically?

You want to be able to review it in about ten minutes—

no more than that. You don't want to get to where you're over thinking it. Obviously, the night before, you want to read through the script a couple of times. You want to have the read-through take only about ten to twelve minutes, focusing on certain things that motivate and inspire you. These are the things that get you into a good state of mind. You also want to read your script right before you head out to the match, so that when you do get called to the court, the script feels fresh in your mind.

Like thirty minutes before a match? An hour? Two hours?

I'd say closer to thirty minutes before the match. If you do it two hours before you play, then it may not be that fresh when you're walking onto the court. You could certainly skim through it two hours before, but you want a good reading of the script so you hear it in your mind right before you go on. So, I'd say read it within thirty minutes.

After a player has lost a tough point, how do you recommend they get their mind back into focus?

I like the saying, "Flush it." Saying that makes you laugh and keeps you relaxed at the same time. You can't avoid playing a bad point in tennis. There are so many points and so many opportunities for us to make mistakes. It's not a sport that makes it easy to be perfect. It's a very difficult sport, so you're going to make some mistakes. The first thing is to tell yourself to flush it and move forward. This tells our mind to get rid of that mistake or that point that we don't like. I'm flushing it, I'm getting rid of it, and then I'm moving forward to look ahead.

I tell a lot of my juniors and pros, "Remember, it's one point." It may be a critical point, or it may not be, but at the end of the day, what's it costing you? It's costing you one point. If you mentally flush it, hopefully you can laugh at the same time, keep yourself relaxed, and move forward.

I've done a lot of these interviews, and everyone has different answers. You'd think everyone would say the same thing, but each coach has different ideas.

The beautiful part about the mental game—which I love; it's my niche—is we all have our information on how to teach, how to get people relaxed, and how to get them ready to deal with certain issues and different styles of play and strokes. We're unique individuals, so each coach is going to be different because our communication tools and how we get our message across to the players are so different. If you're teaching two people how to play tennis, you might tell them the same exact thing in terms of, "You need to hit your forehand low to high across your body." However, you're going to explain it and demonstrate it visually in a different way to each player. So it can come across differently even though it's the same concept.

Say, its match point and championship point. How does a player keep themselves calm and focused?

That's a great question and it refers to one area where I think I helped Bob and Mike, the Bryan brothers. When I first started coaching them in 2003, they had lost a couple of tough matches when they had served for the match and they had also not won their first slam or finished number one yet. So, they hadn't had that positive experience. It's the old saying, "If you're interviewing for a job, how do you get the experience if you don't have the experience?" You've got to start having it at some point. How do you get the confidence if you haven't been through that situation?

One thing I told them was, "Walk up to the line if you're serving or if it's break point. Try to close out the point or the match and really own it." Own the situation, and then it's okay to be nervous. Own the fact that you have some nerves, but own the situation and say, "You know what? This is my situation and I'm going to go out and get it." A lot of the time we step into a situation with the mindset that we hope it works out. When we only hope it works out, we become very tentative and try to play it very safe. By stepping up to that line, so to speak, you're making the statement that you want to close out the match. You basically own it and say, "This is my opportunity and I'm going to really take it by concentrating on hitting a big serve or getting to the net. This is what my game plan is dictating and it's been working." You must really believe that you're going to do it and get the win, rather than playing it safe and hoping not to lose. I know we've heard that a lot, but you want to own the situation. You need to say, "This is where I'm at, and I'm going to get it rather than just waiting for it and hoping it will happen."

I guess it's all about believing in your strengths and game plan and being proactive in making it happen?

Yes. Focus on your strengths. That was my second part. Focus on your style of play and your game plan. You mentioned a big serve. Right now, I'm coaching Sam Querrey. He needs to think about standing up tall and hitting a big serve. When you make that big serve, all of a sudden you're thinking about your weapons, and that makes you feel good. It takes away pressure and helps alleviate stress because you're thinking about your weapons and what makes you win. Focus on what your game plan is and what you do really well. That helps to take away thoughts of, "Am I going to win or am I going to lose?" You want to think about what you're trying to execute, not the result.

In a long rally, obviously the person who keeps their focus longer will win. What are your secrets for players to really stay focused throughout the whole point?

Can you state that question one more time?

Let's take, for example, Nadal. No matter how long the point is, he's in the zone for the whole point. How does one stay in that sort of mindset and not lose focus throughout the point?

I think with somebody like that, it's your upbringing. It goes back to your style of play. Nadal isn't tall or a big guy, so he constantly has to work points. He's played on clay, which makes you more patient with your game but also with your mind, your focus. It's all about how you train and prepare yourself throughout the years before you turn pro. It's about your style of play. If you're a counter-puncher, or more of a baseline attacker, then you train for that type of game. For example, Sam Querrey has a huge serve, a huge forehand, and he's 6' 6"." Today, we trained for four hours. We weren't training to stay three feet behind the base line or hit ten feet above the net or off the back foot with a lot of spin. In that four-hour training, we were focusing on his huge serve, on first-strike tennis, on offense beginning with the first ball, because of his size. With any player, you have to ask: What's his style of play, what's he good at?

To go back to your question, with guys like Nadal who are constantly grinding out the point, a lot of their focus is built from all the training and hours they've put in. That's why they can get their mind to focus for that long. It's tough. They do a really good job of flushing and letting go of the nerves and their thoughts. They take some deep breaths and use the time in between their points. You have to let go in between or you can't last for very long. You'll burn yourself out.

What's the secret to bringing out inner confidence in a player?

It's necessary for a player to communicate where they're at, to be open about it, and talk with their trainer or their coach or their sports psychologist about it. You need to talk to somebody who understands the sport. You need to say to them, "I'm just not feeling very confident. I haven't been winning a lot of matches lately," or, "I'm feeling great on my forehand and I feel good about this match." A lot of us tend to want to hide what we're thinking and feeling and not talk about it, especially when we're not feeling good and we're not confident.

When we discuss the mental game, we talk about strategy and we talk about forehand and footwork all the time, but it's become more popular and more okay to talk about mindset and dealing with stress and nerves. Confidence is such a big thing in tennis because in singles, it's one on one. You're out there and not getting any coaching in the performance or during the match, so it's up to you. You have to communicate in order to understand where you are with your game right now. It doesn't matter what your rank or level is, whether it's pro, college or junior. You can lose your confidence very, very quickly. It happens to all of us. It happened to Agassi, it happens to Federer, and it happens to Serena Williams. You have to communicate about your mental state. You need to have scripts and affirmations that make you feel good about yourself and about your game. You need to revisit those scripts. You don't read them just once. Just like when you're playing tennis, you've got to keep training during your off weeks and off seasons. The same thing is true with your mind. You've got to train it and, like anything else, repetition is the key. You have to keep repeating those things that make you feel good.

What's the most important thing to think about during a changeover?

That's another really good question. There are different theories. You can use that time to flush any thoughts and to be honest with yourself. If there are positive thoughts going on, if you're in the lead, then you're doing well and it's good to keep those positive thoughts. You tell yourself, "I'm serving really well." If it's a close match or maybe you aren't playing well, you have to flush negative thoughts and, a lot of the time, you need to keep the switch turned off. Don't think. Use that time to towel off, to hydrate, to relax, and, more than anything, to keep yourself calm. In most cases, I'd say to take the time off, like you're taking the day off at work. Take the time off, really let your body cool down, and let your mind rest. When you get back out there—like we talked about with Nadal—then you're back at work.

In tennis, there's so much thinking and analyzing going on with every single shot and especially nowadays, there's a strong focus on strategy. There's so much to the game of tennis—angles and spins—you have to give your mind a chance to breathe, so to speak, and relax.

You don't recommend people think about strategy during the changeover?

You know, I don't. It's okay to revisit your game, but I feel that if you do, then you're constantly thinking about strategy. If things aren't working and you need to revisit, it's good to just let yourself relax for that 90 seconds. If things aren't working and you're frustrated, flush the thoughts and try to move forward. When you move forward, try to think, "What can I do? What would work against this type of player?" Maybe you look back over the game and recognize your serve-and-volley game isn't working, so maybe you need to stay back and make your opponent play.

There are definitely times when you need to revisit your game and go to plan B or adjust a little bit. But most of the time, you want to use the changeover to keep yourself calm and quiet mentally. Flip the switch off for a little bit and let your mind take a break.

Butterflies and nerves have the ability to be a positive force if channeled correctly. Do you have a method to help players figure out how to channel all that energy positively?

Go ahead and own the nerves. Just accept it. The reason I say that is because it's impossible to avoid nerves. They're always going to be there. There are ways to control them better, decrease the amount or the time that they happen, but, in my opinion, there isn't a remedy that promises you'll never get nervous. In fact, you hear a lot of players say, "It's probably good that I was a little nervous going into the match." That feeling, especially for professionals, lets them know they're ready to do battle. Owning it and accepting it is the key. "I'm going to be nervous and it's okay because my opponent is probably nervous too. Being nervous means I'm getting ready to go into battle."

The second thing, which relates to the channeling that you asked about, is to understand that the nervousness is there. The player needs to remember to relax and let go with their footwork, with their breathing, or with their stroke, because nerves trap us mentally and they trap our nervous system and our breathing. They trap our ability to let the stroke go. When that happens, the player doesn't finish the

"I'm going to be nervous and it's okay because my opponent is probably nervous too. Being nervous means I'm getting ready to go into battle."

spin and the ball goes everywhere. I always tell my players, "Trust your system of play." If you're hitting the chip, if you're hitting the driving forehand, if you're hitting the backhand down the line or the top spin, let it go. Trust the system and try to channel it through "Here's what I do, whether I'm nervous, whether I'm really nervous, whether I'm not nervous at all, or whether I'm over-confident."

Whatever the emotion is, try to trust your system, the intention of what you're trying to do. Let the shot go, because you've already recognized that you own it. "Okay, I'm nervous. I know it. I know what I need to do, so I'm going to make sure I really commit and trust my system; trust the shot that I'm hitting."

I haven't heard anyone talk about this, and I'd like to know what you think. Let's say you're about to get up to return serve and you're really nervous. It's a big point and you have butterflies. Would it be helpful to jump up and down, get yourself hyped up, to get the energy flowing a little more?

Yes, absolutely. As you know well, attention to movement has become a big part of tennis. When I coached Bob and

Mike Bryan for those three years, one thing that was amazing was how jumping up and down really helped them get rid of nerves. They'll tell you, they just kept bouncing. That's why they're still always bouncing.

That's a good point. I didn't even think about that.

The cool thing about them being identical twins is that they're always hopping together and in unison. The bouncing helps decrease the nerves, which are hard to get rid of, even if you're the best doubles team in history. They still have them. When you're moving, you tend not to think too much about negative outcomes. There's a positive energy, as you said, that derives from realizing "I'm active, I feel good, I'm bouncing, I'm moving." You relax more when you move and your mind goes more to the positive. It's just a good feeling when you're bouncing. On the other hand, when you get stagnant or flatfooted, you feel frozen. The nerves get you, and that's when you start thinking about "What ifs" and "I hopes" instead of, "I'm going to..." and "I'm good." So yes, the bouncing and all the movement before you settle into the point is very good.

In your opinion, what's the difference between a professional player that remains at a rank of 50 to 100 in the world most of their career and the player that's in the top 20? Most are talented and most are hardworking, so, what would you say is the big difference?

There are a few things, which I'm going to mention but not necessarily in order. One is having a weapon. The more consistent players have a weapon they can rely on to make the points and the wins much more efficient and easier. This weapon is reliable, day in and day out. A big serve or a big forehand is such a weapon. Roger has an amazing ability to time the ball early, he has a wicked forehand, and he has a very good serve that he can place. These are weapons that help him win matches very efficiently, which means he's really consistent from week to week. Having a weapon, whether it's a big forehand or a big serve—which are the two main ones, nowadays—is vital. Any sort of weapon—movement, a backhand down the line, something that really distinguishes you—that's critical.

Movement is a big part of what makes a player great. If you look at the players in the top ten or top twenty, the majority of them move really, really well. Again, moving well obviously makes it easier for them to get to the ball, execute their shots, and get to their weapon so they can use that forehand if they need to and run around the backhand. They can get up to the short ball or get back to deeper balls and play good defense. Movement is so important because it helps you get to your weapon and play your game.

The last thing is having the ability to let go. You look at Djokovic, you look at Nadal, and you look at Azarenka and you see they have an amazing ability to let go. As I was saying earlier, even when the match is extremely close, when they're not playing well, when they're not hitting their weapon or playing a particular shot very well or their serve is poor, they can let it go. They have this amazing ability, even at crunch time. They have the ability to continue to deal with the nerves in a way that they're able to trust their system and fully commit to each shot. An example of this ability to let go after a bad shot is swinging through the ball and hitting the serve at 135 miles an hour, just like they've been doing the whole match. They have an amazing ability to keep themselves calm, not get caught up too much in thinking about the result—those thoughts of "I might miss this or I could lose this point" —and trusting their game: "This is what I do and I'm going to continue to do it, even though it's the biggest point of the match." That's really difficult, when you boil it all down.

What's your advice to young players who dream of being a professional tennis player but don't think they have what it takes?

My advice to them is find players who've been in their same situation, or research and read stories about players in that situation. A good example is Sam Querry, the guy I just signed on to coach full time. Here's a guy that was a good junior and signed on to play at USC. He'd already committed and already signed. He played three future events, which are lower tier tournaments, before he was about to play at USC. He lost the first round, in all three. He got a wild card in one of the local tournaments and played two challengers, which is, in terms of the tiers, much more difficult. He ended up winning both the challengers.

He started by playing futures, which is the beginning level, and lost the first round. Who would have thought that he'd win two challengers, which are much higher tier tournament levels—and then go on to be ranked 17 in the world? Originally, he'd only been thinking of pursuing college tennis.

I always say that everybody's path is so unique and so different. You have to work hard, you have to have faith, you have to have a good team around you, you have to roll with the punches, and you have to recognize your path is unique. I think too many times players copy other peoples' plans. You have to go with what plan is in front of you and realize that there are so many different paths to get to the goal. Find examples of people that have different paths. Sampras' path was different than Courier's, which was different than Sam Querrey's, which was different than Nadal's, who was taught by his uncle. That would be my advice. Understand your path. It's unique. Don't get down.

There are many ways to get there. Research it. Listen to stories. They can be very motivating.

What's the trick for junior players to create and foster a healthy tennis attitude on a consistent basis?

The most important thing is having a really good team around you and somebody that you feel comfortable communicating with, because tennis is a very, very difficult sport. If you're in juniors and are serious, hopefully you're playing a hundred matches a year. I don't know how many weeks that would be, but if you're playing a lot of matches, you get the benefit of all that experience. There's only one winner every single week, so the reality is that with a 128 draw or a 64 draw, there are 127 people in the first case and 63 in the second that are going to lose at some point. You need to see the big picture of what you're developing and where your game is going. You should have short-term and long-term goals, and you should revisit them often so that you can understand where you are and where your progress has occurred. This brings about a good balance, and that's the key.

You need to have a good team around you; a coach that you can talk with about things, including the mental side of the game; a good sports psychologist that can help you understand and deal with some of the stresses; parents that are there for you no matter what; and a team around you that makes the game fun and enjoyable. You need these things because it's a long road. If you have a good team around you that you can communicate with and with whom you can share the ups and the downs—of which there are a lot in tennis—then you have a good, balanced team and the junior player will have a good, balanced mind. When you have good people around you and balance, it creates good things in your world and in your head.

You have a healthy approach to your day-in-and-day-out practices and matches.

What do you recommend that a junior player who has professional aspirations and is practicing and playing a lot of tournaments do to keep a balanced life?

Early on, I don't think it's necessary to do anything in particular. Again, every path is different. I'm not one who thinks you can play only tennis from age five to when you're 18. There are sports, like soccer, that can help you learn some aspects of the game. Obviously, as you get older—say 13, 14, 15, 16—it becomes more about the value of time. From ages 4 to 10, having a healthy balance means trying other activities and finding out what you like to do. Maybe it's movies, maybe it's a hobby, maybe it's remote-control airplanes. Whatever it is.

Bob and Mike were very much into music and learned how to play guitar, drums, and keyboard, with their parents' help. I think that gave them a really nice outlet. If they had a bad loss, they didn't sit in their room and moan, "Oh my gosh, I've got nothing." They said, "Let's go play some music, let's go jam out." It was an outlet for them, a way for them to get away from the tennis world and let their mind relax and focus on something different. I think that's really healthy. The two outlets I see the most on the tour are music and golf. I see more players who are learning an instrument and they bring it on the road with them—a guitar, drums, or a keyboard. Golf is relaxing and it's peaceful. Marty Fish is a very good golfer. Tim Henman, Sampras, Sam Querrey, and John Isner play golf. Bob and Mike didn't go golfing a lot, but we played music probably every day. We'd go back to the hotel room and play some music or listen to music. I found that interesting. Those are the two outlets that the pros like. Maybe more juniors should participate in these outlets.

We talked a little bit about goals before, but are there any specific goal-setting practices that you recommend for junior players?

It's good to have four or five short-term goals. When I say short-term, I mean something like this: I'll say, "Okay, 'John' what do you want to accomplish by the end of the summer?" The goals are even more short-term in our junior program. Our junior program runs from five to seven in the evening. For example, I might say, "What do you want to accomplish? It's five o'clock right now. What's one of the goals you want to reach by seven o'clock?" Or, "It's our last hour of juniors. At six o'clock we're going to play sets. In this set, what's your goal? Give me a couple of goals, we'll ask the kids." One response might be, "Well, I want to get my first-serve percentage up." That's a great goal. "I want to cut down on my mistakes and see if I can keep six balls in play." That's really good. "I want to actually put more returns in play." Okay, that's great. Short-term goals can be set for that hour, for that week, or for over the course of the summer.

It's necessary to have some longer-term goals as well. We develop a strategy and figure out how we think we're going to accomplish it, based on the style of play, the player's weapons, and his game. The most important thing is to write these down in a tennis notebook.

I like to have all my juniors and all my players have a tennis notebook, which can be any sort of notebook. Write on it Sam's Tennis Notebook or whatever and have different tabs in there. Have a goals tab that lists short- and long-term goals. Revisit these every few days, a couple times a week. Have certain times that you pick up the book and ask yourself, "Did I accomplish my goal for this day or for this week?" or "It's summer and we're in late August. Let's see how I did." Highlight the goals, scratch them off, write through them, or check them off. Have a system you like that lets you know, "I accomplished that goal, I can let that one go, I can knock that one off." The goals that aren't checked off are the ones you need to focus on for next time. Don't just set goals at one session or for one time and the next year you don't have any. You've got to keep setting new goals. This makes you raise the bar, so to speak, and strive to be better.

How often did you say you should keep looking at the list of goals? Every day or every week?

Obviously, it depends. Your short-term goals are set every week, so you want to look at them every day and see how you're doing and if you're getting closer to meeting them. At the end of the year, you might revisit long-term goals like that to get you motivated. And maybe you look at them once or twice throughout the week. You want the goals, even the long-term goals, to be fresh in your brain. "Here's what I'm working toward," If you've given yourself a year to accomplish it, you don't have to cram it into your brain every single day.

You'd get overwhelmed, I guess.

Yes. Like I said, if you set a goal for this week, then you might look at that each day and ask yourself, "Am I getting better on my first-serve percentage?" Tomorrow you ask, "Did I do better than yesterday?" Now you've only got five days left. If your first-serve percentage is a goal for the year, then I don't think you need to look at it every day. Maybe you look at it once a week or six to eight times a month or something like that.

How do you push the players when they don't feel like training?

If they don't feel like training, I'd look at what work has been put in. Have they played a ton of matches? Have they traveled a lot? Have they been practicing a crazy amount of time in a given time span? They may need some time off. I don't think coaches value how critical time off is. Not just for the player's body because it's such a physically demanding sport, but also to refresh their battery, their mind, their energy level, and their spark. I think its okay to get away from the game and take time off to recharge the battery. I also think that if you're tired, there are other ways you can train for the game.

For a junior player, my advice is to take him to a local college match, to provide side-door motivation. You motivate them without them even knowing, train them without them knowing. Tennis is very repetitive: You go out, you warm up for fifteen minutes, you hit your volley, and you hit your serves. You're hitting the same tennis ball and the same lines. You have to break it up. Go to a pro match. Go to a Davis Cup match. Do something where you're not physically taxing your body or your mind, and it's something a little bit different.

The other thing, which is up to the coach and the family, is to make sure the practices have a plan and that you mix it up a little. Obviously, you have to work on strengths and weaknesses, and you have a game plan that focuses on how to work on the player's style of play. But you have to make it fun. Play games, mix up hitting partners, do different drills, and try not to get stuck in the same routine. It's very easy for all of us to do that, whether it's the coach or the player. Go to a different site, maybe hit on clay. Just try to mix it up so it doesn't get stagnant.

What skills should the serious tennis player hope to gain and take away from living a tennis-focused life?

That's a good one. Tennis is a one-on-one, combat sport, so you learn survival, fighting, and creative thinking skills. If you ride a bike, there's thought that goes into it if you're serious. You have to think so much more as a pro athlete, whether you're a cyclist or baseball player or whatever. In tennis, you're out there on your own. There's no coaching. You really have to be independent. You have to be your own coach when you're in a match. You have to keep yourself calm and, as I said, you have to draw on your creative thinking. The ability to solve problems and come up with solutions in a very short amount of time is a great skill. The ability to handle stress, handle nerves, learn strategies and game plans to try to deal with challenges, and to succeed at the game is a very good skill. Learning how to keep yourself relaxed and calm is another skill that tennis teaches.

I'll say this to finish up. Communication skills are so important. I know I've talked about that several times, but you build some amazing contacts and relationships through tennis, and they're relationships that last a long time. I feel tennis players are very good with people, overall. The majority of them communicate well. They're humble because they really know how hard tennis is and how much work it takes physically, emotionally, and mentally. Relationships are so big, from your coach to your parents. You learn to respect sportsmanship through the one-on-one battles with your opponents. You learn how to deal with all kinds of people.

Last question; who are your role models in the game of tennis?

That's a really good question. I have a couple of answers. When I was growing up, I really admired Stefan Edberg. I loved how graceful he was playing the game and his sportsmanship. Talk about a guy that I felt handled himself really well. He was competitive and wanted to win more than anybody, but he was very humble. I liked the way he carried himself so calmly when he entered the court. I looked up to him a lot.

Andre Agassi is another role model. When I got to know him personally, I learned about everything he'd gone through and his perspective on the game, on life, on family, and how those things transformed him. I saw how he was always looking to be not just a better tennis player but a better person.

And then Rod Laver, he's a guy who's still around and could easily brag about his skills: "If I'd been able to play, man, I'd have all those slams." He just loves the game. He loves Federer, he loves Nadal, and he loves tennis. He's such a humble and great man. He's so complimentary of everybody, whether you're ranked 100 in the world or number 1. His attitude is so great for the game, and I really admire him.

The last thing I want to say is that whoever I'm coaching, I look up to them, but in a different way. I'm coaching them, running the practices, and getting them ready for their matches, but I really admire the battles they go through and the challenges they face. They travel many weeks throughout the year. They miss their families and deal with tough losses during many of those weeks, because most people don't win every week. As with the Bryans, I really admire that. As a coach, it's important to understand what they're going through and respect that. They can feel your respect. It lets them know they're worth your efforts and that you believe in them.

This is how I feel about the Bryan Brothers. We worked together for three years and have maintained a professional relationship and close friendship for twelve years. I admire how hard they work, how professional they are, and how much they give back to the fans and this great sport. They are the greatest doubles team in history and more importantly they are humble and amazing people. I really admire them for that.

Ellis Ferreira:

Former number-one doubles player
in the world

Ellis Ferreira

Former number-one doubles player in the world

To begin, please tell me what some of your pre-match rituals were when you were playing.

The important thing I always tried to do was keep my personality. A lot of players change their normal personalities when they go out on the court. What I found was that I am an outgoing guy and when I try to get a little too serious before matches I tend to be more nervous on the court. But when I stayed nice and loose before a match, I was able to play loose on the court.

You know, everyone is different, but I saw that people's personalities are typically the same on and off the court. If they are intense people off the court, they're normally intense on the court. But if they're relaxed off the court, they're more than likely relaxed on the court. So I just try to stay loose—I kind of behave like its any regular day, and I try to go out there and have fun.

After you lose a tough point, how do you get yourself back into a good mindset?

A lot of that is really a learned behavior and it is a very tough thing to do. I think that returning to a good mindset is achieved through trial and error, but eventually you learn how to just let go of whatever is bothering you.

One of the things that I learned how to do was just to play more in the moment and not let the disappointment of losing the last point get into my mind. If you do that, your mind then wanders into, "Well, now I'm going to lose the game, and if I lose the game I'll lose my serve, and if I lose my serve I'll lose the match." It's more than just a temporary type of thing. So I tell myself, "You lost the point and that's disappointing, but let's move on to the next point." Once you understand how your thoughts can easily string together in a negative way, you start to learn that you need to let go.

Let's say you're coaching someone and they're having difficulty getting back into a positive frame of mind. What do you do to help them change that behavior and figure out how to let it go?

A lot of it is appealing to an almost psychological discussion of "If you don't let it go, then what happens next, and then what happens next, and then what happens next?" If you can appeal to some sort of logical understanding of where negative thoughts lead, then hopefully the player will come to the same conclusion that it's not really productive, and in 25 seconds there's another point to play. I tell them to always take a towel onto the court so that they can go back to the towel or do some other activity that will get their mind off the fact that they may have missed a shot.

Let's say its match point or championship point. How do you tell your students to stay calm?

If you're up match point, then the other person is under a tremendous amount of pressure as well. So putting the ball in play and forcing the other person to play the point is a good way to get around that.

If you put the ball in play and the other person hits a good shot and you lose that point, then unfortunately there's nothing you can do about that. But if you don't put the ball in play, then you're going to give the point away easily. So focus on doing what is actually in your control, and that is getting that ball into that box and into the court to the best of your ability. Whatever happens after that, don't sweat it, because at the end of the day you don't have much control over it anyway.

When you played professionally, did any of your peers use footwork exercises, such as jumping up and down or some other form of exercise, to get out of the funk of thinking about what might have just happened in the game? Do you recommend a particular ritual every time?

Well, I think everybody is going to have their own little thing that calms them down. Having some sort of ritual is very helpful because it gets you into familiar territory that can calm and slow you down. That's why I stress going to the towel. Sometimes that works well and it slows you down and allows you to think about what you want to do next.

You were number one in doubles at one time, correct?

Yes, in 2000.

What do you think was the difference between you and your partner and the rest of the field when you were number one? Because I find most of the time when I ask this question,

players say everyone's working hard, everyone's talented, but there is just a certain level of confidence that makes the difference. I'm just wondering if that was true with you?

I definitely remember having this feeling that I was going to win. No matter what the score was, I would just figure somehow we were going to pull it out—the other guys would choke, something would happen.

I always say that winning and losing are habits. So when you start losing, it becomes a habit, but when you start winning, winning also becomes a habit. There were so many matches that we squeaked out, or we pulled out, that you just got this feeling that you were going to win. You didn't know how, or what the score was, or what it was going to be, but you knew, "At the end of this match, we're going to win it."

It was just because when push came to shove we were probably going to focus more on getting the ball in play, where the other guys, more than likely, were going to focus on "Oh my goodness, we're almost about to beat these guys." And you learn so much on the journey to get to the top 10 position from 50/60; you understand that things can change so quickly. A lot of times people think, "Hey, we're going to win," and then all of a sudden they lose. Whereas the guys at the top are not really thinking about whether they're going to win or lose, they're just playing, and suddenly things turn their way and they're not surprised by it.

I just got into that situation where I had so much confidence in our ability to make the shots when it counted that I just knew that somehow we were going to pull this thing out.

Like when I play ping pong. *[Laughing]*

You know, you just don't panic. There's so much more

to play, and it's one thing to go up a set and a break and another thing to close it out. We knew we were definitely going to make our shots and we were going to put the other guys under a lot of pressure, and more often than not the other guys were going to buckle.

What do you think is the most important thing to think about during a changeover, especially if you're a junior player?

I think the most important thing to ask yourself is, "Who is doing what to whom?" That's always been really important. You've got to understand what is going on.

If you've won the first set, what have you been doing in order to win that first set? Sounds logical, but if you're doing something right you need to keep doing it. So you've got to keep reminding yourself, "Hey, looks like this is working, we're up a break, that's great. All right, now we're up two breaks—wow, this is really working, and that's great. We need to keep working the backhand, we need to keep running this person, we need to keep pressuring them," whatever it is, so that you can continue doing those things.

And then if you're losing, you've also got to look at what is going on. "Why are we losing? Do we have a good idea, a good plan that we're not executing and so we need to concentrate harder, or is coming to the net and rushing this person not working? They just love the target and are eating us alive."

So, it's very, very important that you take stock of what's actually going on. Sometimes players don't take the time to actually reflect on that.

Concerning butterflies and nerves, they can either slow a person down, make you flat-footed, or you can channel them to be really energizing. Do you have any tricks that you recommend players should due to channel their nervousness correctly?

Well, I think the big thing to understand is that there is a difference between butterflies and being nervous.

Butterflies just mean the excitement and anticipation of battle. Nerves mean that you actually have the wrong strategy to start with. There is a big, big difference. When a professional goes out there he knows that tennis is not about him. Tennis is about his opponent. If his opponent isn't equal to the challenge today, the pro knows he's going to obliterate him.

If you make tennis about yourself, you're nervous about whether or not you're going to be able to hit the winners or do the thing that you're trying to do. Whereas having butterflies is just being excited about getting out there. Butterflies don't last very long. That's why we say they're butterflies. It's not like saying they're bees or hornets. Butterflies make it sound like it's quite easy to get rid of them, so I think that's a good term.

So nerves and butterflies are very, very different. And when I was playing, once I got good, I never got nervous. I had butterflies, I was excited about getting out there, but I wasn't nervous because I knew that we had a good strategy. We were going to put our opponents under pressure, but it wasn't a strategy of "We're going to hit three winners down the line and ace them every time." That would make me nervous.

I guess it's all about preparation at that point?

Yeah, well you know, when you interview the pros before they play they seem fairly calm and relaxed. They're excited about getting out there and competing but they don't look nervous. They're going to hit their shots, and they're going to put their opponents under pressure. They're not intending to hit winners. If the other guy doesn't get to it, that's not the pro's fault.

Alright, for all the junior players out there that dream of being professionals, but lack the self belief that they can make it happen, what sort of advice do you have for them to help them gain belief in themselves?

Again, don't make tennis about you. Make tennis about your opponent. Work very hard on bringing something to the table. Whether you're someone who likes to come to the net or are very physical and likes to hit to the open court and run someone. Put pressure on your opponent.

Make sure that you have a strong identity and understand who you are and what you offer as a tennis player. So then you can turn that around and say, "Alright, I'm confident in what I do, this game is not about me." When you make tennis about yourself, there are a lot of nerves about being able to actually execute this difficult thing that you're trying to do. You're putting all the pressure on yourself.

So, before you even go out there, you're already nervous, thinking, "Geez, I hope I can hit a winner in the first two shots—this guy looks pretty athletic. I mean, what if I don't hit a winner in the first two shots?" So confidence can be eroded very quickly before you even start. Even if you have a strategy, it becomes almost impossible to execute. So, the best advice is to try to play as many points as possible, as many practice matches and competitions as possible. You've got to compete.

Can you describe your first experience playing under the lights at the US Open?

I think it was a mixed doubles match. Obviously, you get scared with all the lights, and just getting out there is very intimidating, but once you settle in and concentrate on what you're doing, it gets a lot better. It was definitely exciting. It was a wonderful experience where you really get forced to have to focus on the small things. You know, first serve, first ball, make the return, get it past the guy and then simplify it down. So it's a really good learning experience.

Did you enjoy looking up, looking around at the people?

Yeah, that was pretty exciting. You start thinking to yourself, "Okay, I could get used to this." I love the stage; I definitely am a person who enjoyed playing on the biggest stage. And when you hit a good shot, you feel the energy of the crowd. That's when I kind of realized: "I could be pretty good at this."

How do you recommend junior players keep a balanced life but still have an appropriate emphasis on their tennis?

Obviously it's subjective for each person, but I mean for the players who are really shooting for something professionally.

I guess the best advice is that they need to follow a series of steps. You know, you go to school, you go to sixth grade, and then when you do well in sixth grade they pass you on to seventh grade, and then when you go to seventh grade, you do well and they move you to eighth—same with tennis there are logical steps to how tennis works.

In Florida we have super series events, and in the Southeast they have the Bullfrogs. You've got to go from those levels and then to the regionals. Start doing well there and get some success, and from there play some national events and some national opens and win some nationals at that level. I think that each level you're able to master gives you a kind of battle scar and you begin believing that you belong in the sport.

You know that you belong because you've earned the right to get into the next tournament. I'm not a big fan of wild cards unless they're performance-based, unless you've won a tournament or done something good and you now deserve, through that performance, to get into a tournament. Just because you're a nice kid or somebody thinks you're good, I wouldn't take a wild card because you have to feel like you belong there and that you've got the battle scars just like everybody else.

Slowly, then, you move your way up. If you're doing well, you're doing well. Our sport's performance-based foundation is black and white: either you have the ranking and the results, or you don't. But so often I see a lot of juniors saying, "You know, I'm really good." Well, how many tournaments have you won? What's your ranking? "Well, I haven't played much, but I'm really good." My reaction is, "From what I see, you're this or that."

So focus more on the performance end of it. If you win and you do well on one level, then move to the next, and after that one move to the next.

When did you realize you were pretty good at this sport and you could make a potential career out of it?

Well, I was in South Africa and I had a high ranking every year. I was top five in the country in the juniors. Again, that was based on performance.

You were top 5 starting in the 12's or the 14's . . ?

Oh no. It was more like in the 16's. In the 12's anyone can be good. I saw that from my brothers. I guess I was advised well that in the 12's anyone could win. But, once you get a little bit older, everyone kind of grows up.

In the 12's, I'm telling you, there were a lot of people who weren't winning all the time. *[Laughing]*

Right, and that's the thing: Sometimes there are youngsters in the 10's and 12's and even sometimes in the 14's who realize that they aren't competitive by the time they get into the 16's and 18's. Maybe they were a little bit bigger than their opponents at the lower levels.

Anyway, I didn't do very well in the 12's. I was very erratic and there were a lot of younger, smaller guys that were very steady. I would lose matches 0-0, 1 and 1, 2 and 2. But as I got a little bit stronger, all of a sudden I was able to overpower them.

So when I started doing well in the 16's, I started to realize, "I'm pretty good at tennis."

Did you use any sort of goal-setting practices throughout your career, or do you recommend any for junior players?

I set some a goal for myself in the juniors of going to America on a tennis scholarship. That was a big goal of mine. I believe in goals, they're very important. You have to set goals that are attainable—short-term, long-term goals.

It's just very difficult to progress without really knowing where you're supposed to go. Goals are important, but they've got be based on some sort of reality too. I had a goal to get a scholarship to go to university and then I had a dream of being a professional tennis player. But the path that I was on wasn't taking me to a professional career because guys like Wayne Ferreira, and other guys, they were whacking me easy. I knew, realistically, I just wasn't as good as those guys, which was fine.

So I created a different goal for myself, something I thought was attainable, which was a scholarship to a university to get an education and to continue my tennis. Then all of a sudden one day I'm standing on the court with Wayne Ferreira and we're playing for the Davis Cup or we're in the Olympics. I was like, "Wow, how did I get here?" I took a different path but ended up in the same place he did.

Besides just stating what your goals were, did you use any sort of very specific methodology to get yourself moving from step to step or would you recommend any?

Well, it's one thing to make a goal. Now we're going

to say, "How do we actually achieve that goal?" For example, you're going to have to work a little harder if you're going to have to get into better shape. You've got to have specific things that are going to help you do that. Those are important, and they've got to be realistic. You've got to say, "Hey, can I improve this, can I work out harder, can I spend more time on the tennis court, can I do this, can I do that?" Otherwise, your goals are kind of not worth the paper they're written on, if you're not prepared to do the things that are going to make those goals reachable.

How did you deal with those moments where you were just burned out from practicing? How did you overcome them?

I just got away from tennis for a while. I recharged my batteries. I tried to take some time off and remember why I was playing tennis in the first place. That's very important.

We all get burned out once in a while but typically that doesn't last very long. We usually are able to look back and think, "Okay, why am I on this journey?" I was on my journey because I was trying to get a scholarship to America, I was trying to get out of South Africa and have a better life. Or I was doing this because I was trying to become a professional tennis player and get to Wimbledon, that was my dream, or to the US Open. You need some time to reflect and get back on track with regard to "What is the goal? What is the point? Why am I doing this? Why am I putting myself through this?" Then you think, "Oh, okay—for that. Is that worth fighting for?" And you respond, "Yup! Alright, let's get back out there."

Last question for you... How have your professional skills— becoming trained and working hard to become a professional tennis player—translated into your personal life? And what would you recommend for players to gain in life skills from their tennis involvement?

Obviously setting goals, and going after those goals, is a good trait to have. Being self-reliant and working hard and not needing someone to lead you by the hand for you to get something done. Getting used to scrapping and doing things on your own. When you're out on the court, there aren't many people who can help you at that point. So people who are successful at this sport clearly have the ability to become successful in other ways on their own.

Tennis players are definitely very confident people. And we're used to scrapping, and clawing, and fighting our way through because that's the only thing we really know how to do. And we're obviously good at it.

Awesome, thank you very much for your time, I appreciate it.

You're welcome.

Luke Jensen:

1993 French Open Doubles Champion with brother Murphy Jensen

ESPN Tennis Analyst since 1994

Syracuse University Head Women's Tennis Coach 2006-2014

Luke Jensen

1993 French Open Doubles Champion with brother Murphy Jensen, ESPN Tennis Analyst since 1994, Syracuse University Head Women's Tennis Coach 2006-2014

What pre-match rituals do you recommend for players to get their heads into the right mindspace before a match?

Everybody—throughout each tournament—is trying to find their best ritual. It starts the night before a match, by being aware of your food, your diet. If you're going to be playing in hot conditions, you're going to have to make sure you're hydrated and eating lots of carbohydrates. If you're indoors or it's cold, you're probably not going to need as many carbohydrates, but you're still going to need to drink a lot. You also need to make sure you take in plenty of electrolytes.

The night before a match, you want to make sure your equipment is ready. Are your racquets gripped right? How many racquets do you have? Do you need to string any racquets? You shouldn't have any surprises with your equipment when match time comes. That racquet is your lifeline. Do you have an extra pair of shoes in your bag in case you need them? What about an extra pair of shoelaces? Make sure you have your water and maybe a banana or something to eat. Make sure you take care of all the little details, and be prepared for the longest match you may ever play in your life.

You have to always prepare for the worst-case scenario. If a player has his water, Gatorade, food, a game plan, and his racquets ready, that settles him down emotionally better than any other aspect of preparation or any words of encouragement. Covering all those bases in advance really helps players be able to focus more on how they can play better. You don't want to be out there thinking, "Oh, I don't have an extra racquet," or, "My grip is slipping and I don't have an extra one." Being confident about all the little details makes a competitor calmer in the chaos of competition.

In addition, whether you know your opponent or not, do you have a game plan for how you want to play and how you want to attack that opponent? Do you have some strategies or some kind of a scouting report on your opponent that's relevant to the attack plan you're about to put in play? This all needs to be considered the night before.

This game is very unique because every point is affected by your opponent—emotionally, tactically, and physically. That's why it's so important to make sure the things you *do* have control of—your equipment, your game plan, and your diet—are ready to go.

The warm-up is a critical consideration. When are you going to warm up and who are you going to warm up with? I see so many players at every level who aren't prepared because they haven't done their homework and the necessary prep leading up to game day. They just kind of show up with mom and dad and begin looking for a practice partner, looking for a practice court and, most of the time, they aren't ready to compete. As a result, there's a great deal of chaos leading up to the match. Therefore, I really promote having the player handle the pre-match prep. I'm not a big fan of having the parents do it, because parents need to play their role and the players have to understand it's *their* match. It's what they want to do, and it's their choice. They need to take ownership of all the little details to prepare for it.

Right before the match, what should a player do to get prepared?

I'm a big fan of music before matches. My siblings and I grew up with the Walkman, the Discman, and the headphones. That all really started in the mid-eighties. I believe that going into competition is like going into a battle or war. When you step into that arena, you need to have a sense of urgency. Your hair should be standing up on the back of your neck. You've got to be so jacked up! I'm a fan of getting into that zone with music.

Everybody has their own ideas about getting psychologically prepared. I like Azarenka's approach right now. She has that hoody thing going and she's got her headphones on. When she walks out onto the court, she's prepared to play her best tennis with the right energy and the right mindset.

Immediately before the match, you definitely need to have a game plan. You need to write it down on a piece of paper, have it with you for any changeovers, and go over it. You need to know what your game plan is, going in. However, as you go through the match, you may have to change that game plan.

After a player loses a tough point, how do you recommend they regain their focus?

There are a lot of ways to go about it. One of the most popular ways now is the "Maria Sharapova" approach, where she turns her back to the court and away from her opponent, away from the match, and just settles in. I was told by Arthur Ashe, years and years ago, when I was a kid, a great way to re-focus is to go to your strings and straighten them.

The big thing that I stress to all my players is to assess the situation right away. I'm not worried if you made the play, missed it, or you choked. I tell them to ask themselves, "What's the situation right now? Am I up a break point or am I down a break point?" Your ability to properly access the situation is going to determine your success.

It's like in football, when a team is down in distance and the clock is running out. You ask yourself, "What kind of play am I about to run?"

If I'm up 40-love, there will be a completely different approach than if I'm down 40-love. Everybody gets wrapped up in "I just lost this point" or "I just missed this shot." I'm not worried about that. I'm worried about what's about to happen in front of me and preparing for it. Once I know the play, I always go to "What would be my adjustment to the forehand I just missed or the backhand I just missed?"

I really stress to my team and my players that if your opponent has hit a great shot, make sure to applaud or tell your opponent, "Great shot." Doing this takes the pressure or the weight off of you, because it creates the thought in your mind that you didn't do anything wrong. When you verbally acknowledge your opponent's great shot or clap your racquet the way some players do, the weight of the pressure of trying to win every point and trying to be perfect lifts.

When you miss a shot, you should be thinking a couple of things: "What's my adjustment? Was it the right tactic?" What we're really looking for is the right tactic combined with the right execution. If you miss the shot, you have to address the tactic first and then understand if it was the right play. For example, did you go right back at your opponent, or were you going to the open court and you just missed the shot? Most of the time you'll see that the player has the right tactic in mind and they're going to the open court, but they just missed the shot. If the missed shot went into the net, then the adjustment is to get underneath the ball next time.

Here's another example: If you hit the ball long due to the wind, then make sure you add more spin next time. Know the answer to the problem. Tennis is just a bunch of problems that our opponents throw at us, that Mother Nature throws at us, or that our emotions throw at us. If we have the answers, it's a lot easier to navigate emotionally through matches. The people who get really bent out of shape and tangled up emotionally are the ones who don't have answers. Say a player double faults, should she think, "So, why did I miss that?" or, "I just stink." Is that really true, that you just stink and that's why you missed that serve? That's being pretty harsh on yourself and I've heard much worse than that! Instead, say to yourself, "Okay, I just didn't put enough top-spin on it, I didn't use my legs, or my adjustment for next time is to snap my wrists." Whatever it is, after thousands and thousands of strokes, you should know the answers to the problems.

Let's say it's match point and championship point. How do you stay calm in a pressure-filled situation like that?

To be perfectly honest, whether it's match point or the first point of the match, I always stress that every point matters. Every point is match point, and there are defining points that will change the dynamic of the match. You could be cheated or you could double fault on match point, but the bottom line is, when you step up to that line to either serve or receive, you've got to have a plan. The players who are hoping, wishing, and praying to win points are going to lose more big points than they win because they're praying that the other side will simply give it to them.

People who win big points—and I've played with some of the best players in the world—always have a plan. They say to themselves, "What do I want to do with my serve and my second shot," or "What do I want to do with this return?" Of course, your plan could change because of your opponent's shot, but at least you walked up to the line with a plan. If you do that with every point, then the preparation you have for each match point is no different than the preparation you have for any other point. You're going to be more successful if you have this understanding.

Remember, match point is just another point in the big, grand scheme of things. Everyone focuses on that match point because it's the final crushing blow. Our sport is unique because we don't have a clock and you truly have to cross the finish line. You've got to win that point or force your opponent into an error. So, however you make it to the end, you can't just drain out the clock to victory. You've got to cross that finish line with strength and confidence!

You should approach every point with a plan that has your strength in mind. Whenever I'm at match point or in a

"You should approach every point with a plan that has your strength in mind."

situation where I'm not playing well, I immediately focus on my strength: "What can I do right now to execute my game plan?" If my opponent beats me, he beats me. Too many people think it's more complicated than it is. All that's necessary is to go out there thinking, "What is my strength and where is their weakness?" I play that scenario and then I see if they can beat me!

How do you continue to improve your concentration throughout a long point so that you can eventually play a long point with the focus that we see in Nadal?

There's no doubt that there's a zone he taps into. If you ever get a chance to watch him practice, you'll see he's in that zone. He could be on court 58 with no one around or he could be on Center Court Wimbledon. His approach is exactly the same, every single time. Too many players, especially junior players, take gaps and huge spaces of time off mentally and they only concentrate when the match is starting to slip away, when the match is getting closer, or when they're starting to play badly.

If you look at the elite players, you'll see they all have different ways to go about their mental game. If you watch the best competitors, such as Djokovic, Sharapova, Serena Williams, or Venus Williams, you'll learn a lot. It doesn't matter if they're playing the first round or a final. They play every point mentally to its maximum, and they also practice that way. They're totally in that zone.

The way Nadal does it; his engine is revved up all the time. That's who he is. He regards every point as a complete and utter battle. He's trying to impose his physicality and mentality on his opponent. It starts with the way he comes out of the tunnel and how he's second to go to the net. He's fixing his water bottles and he's looking to get into the head of his opponents all the time. If you watch him practice, he knows his opponents are watching. He doesn't care about the fans. He wants his future opponents or his next opponent to say that this guy is relentless. If you practice that way, you're going to perform that way. The people that really struggle are the ones who don't make the mental commitment to the idea that every single point and moment—no matter if I'm on the practice court or it's match point—must be played with that winning determination.

It's easy when you're winning to think and play this way, but watch these guys when they're down. That's when the magic truly happens. That's when the coaching, the preparation, and the parenting really kick in. It's not when you're winning! People get that all messed up. It's when you're losing, when you're playing like garbage, the sun is in your eyes, the wind is in your face, and it's raining. When it's cold and you don't care, that's when you're going to reveal everything about your strengths or your weaknesses. When the reality hits you that your game hasn't woken up today, your legs hurt today, or your head is hurting, that's when you should be paying attention. When adversity hits you, what kind of competitor are you? In most instances, when things get tough, most players—no matter how talented—just go away.

Throughout these interviews, one of the main points I've noticed is that when I ask about the difference between the top players and the ones that are a little farther down in the rankings, it becomes clear that everyone is talented and everybody works hard, but the big difference is confidence. How does one gain a higher level of confidence in oneself?

That's a great question. That's always the multi-trillion dollar question. I truly believe that people who win in life, in sports, in business, or in politics are already confident. That started with your coaches, your parents, many, many years ago, who encouraged you when you were losing and cheered you on when you were winning. They always made you feel special, so that when you step on the court today, you have that confidence. And when you step off the court—win or lose—you still have that confidence.

I have to add that I think this word confidence is misdirected. Momentum is the key. Do you have momentum right now, going into this tournament? Do you have momentum going into this match? Consider two opponents stepping onto the court for a match. One has just won 0 and 0, another has won 7 and 6, and a third was down five match points and was down 5-2 in the third, but she came back and won. Logically, you'd think the person winning 0 and 0 is probably going to have more confidence and more momentum. Yes, but I'll tell you, when you come back from match point down or from 5 -2 in the third and win a long, tough match, that creates a different type of momentum. It's almost a bullet-proof, super-hero type of confidence. That's the toughness you need in competition, something that the 0 and 0 match doesn't give you.

I truly believe that confidence has to come from within. Sometimes a concerned parent will say something to me like, "Coach, if you'd coach my son or my daughter, you could give them confidence and you could motivate them. Then they'll be much better." But you know, I don't have a magic wand. The truth is, you either believe in yourself or you don't. There's a great question I always like to ask players, at any age, point blank: "Are you any good?" Now, it's not bragging if you just answer the question. I'll look them straight in the eye and ask, "Are you any good?" They might answer, "Oh, I play tennis good." My question is, "Are you any good?" That's really what I'm asking. When you step up to that net and you're spinning the racquet, you're not asking, "Who's serving and who's receiving?"

You're looking into that person's eyes and you're asking, "Are you any good? Today we're going to find out." If you question yourself when someone comes up to you and says, "Are you any good?" and your answer is something like, "Uh, well..." you need to stop right there. What you should be saying is, "I'm good. Actually, I'm really good, and I'm here to win this tournament and win this match."

As for confidence, if you don't have it, you'll never get it. If you think winning a couple of matches is going to give it to you, then losing a couple of matches is going to take it right away. You're going to ride this roller coaster your whole life. I've never walked into an arena where I didn't think I was the best player in the world, ever! I didn't care if I was a rookie, I didn't care if I was undersized, or if I was injured. I was going out to win because I believed in my ability. That didn't guarantee I was going to win, but it did guarantee I was going to fight until the last swing.

Momentum is the big thing. You see momentum in sports all the time. The New York Giants shouldn't have been in the 2011 NFL playoffs, but they started making a run, they got some momentum, and they won the Super Bowl. In 2011, the St. Louis Cardinals baseball team almost dropped out of the playoff race. They got some momentum, and they won the World Series. It wasn't necessarily that they were the best and most talented team, but they got hot at the right time and that was the key ingredient. They always had confidence. They always believed in themselves. If you don't believe in yourself, you're constantly searching for that belief. If you need someone to give it to you, you'll never win the big one.

What should a player be thinking about during a changeover?

Well, I always break down the "how." How are we winning points? How are we losing points? People want to get wrapped up in the score and how they're playing in the match. The score is just the situation. I'm always stressing, as a player and as a coach, "How am I winning points and how am I losing points?" because you have a mental scoreboard and statistics are changing all the time. The best strategy is to think, "How am I winning points and how am I losing points?" You've got to go to the "How am I winning points?" question to squeeze out those big important points.

Additionally, you somehow have to figure out the solution to "How am I losing points?" in order to fix that area. Too many people get wrapped up in the emotion of the result. They're too results-based. They're stressing out about, "I could lose this match." In your mind, you've already gotten to the end of the match, the end of the process, but you're only at 3-all, 3-4 in the first set! We're just down a set. What are we worried about? The thing about tennis is it's extremely forgiving. You can lose the first set 6-0 and make 50 unforced errors and still come back and win. Whereas in golf, you can play a perfect tournament, get to the last hole, blow up, and lose everything.

I constantly stress that players write in what we call our playbook, which is basically a tennis journal. You should consistently be writing down your thoughts about "How am I winning points, how am I losing points, how do I change these tactics, where's the strength, and where's the weakness?" You, as the player, are a student and a coach of the game. You're right in the middle of this competition, this battle, and you've got to be able to articulate it. If you can't, eventually you're going to come up against some player that's going to make you pay because you're not playing smart tennis. Your approach isn't sound, and it must be!

So, as a player, you have to be doing constant evaluation?

Yes, absolutely! You've got to understand that it's not a case of I'm good, I'm bad, I'm great, or I stink. It's constantly, "How can I get better performance out of my game, out of my mental side, my physical side, and my tactical side?" When the match is over and you lose, you can go cry your eyes out. It should hurt, because you put a lot into it. However, during the match, you don't have time to cry, you don't have time to panic. You only have time to make adjustments.

How do you reboot and refocus when an umpire makes a bad call?

I've never seen an opposing player or an umpire say, "You know what, you're absolutely right. I think I was wrong. I'm going to award you this point." I've never seen that. So, I really stress to my players to move on to the next point. You can challenge it. You can appeal it. But, as soon as it's over, move on!

People get hung up on this call or that call. If the person across the net is calling it close, well, whether it's in junior tennis or college tennis, don't hit it so close. Once it's over, it's done. It can never be changed. There isn't instant replay in the majority of matches that are played. You've got to be able to handle the bad call emotionally and move on, or it will affect your playing.

Additionally, I think parents and coaches allow that behavior when they make comments like, "You know, I can't believe you called that out." The first thing I do, whether it's a match or a practice, is just stomp out that impulse. That's not how you behave in that scenario. You appeal and then you move on. I don't want to hear the drama. I don't want to see you on Broadway looking for an Oscar performance. Move on! It's very important for coaches and parents not to allow that behavior, because once you allow it, it's just going to run rampant and it doesn't help the player.

Butterflies/nerves can either make you focus on not losing or they can fire you up to win. How do you teach your players to take that nervous energy and channel it toward performing better?

The biggest thing I focus on with nerves is to point out that everybody gets nervous. Our coaching staff will show tapes to our players and we'll do a lot of film study on big players in big scenarios where they're serving for matches and you can see they get nervous. In normal tournaments, they're serving and they get nervous. At the 2012 Sony Erickson tournament in Key Biscayne, we saw Nadal blow a match where he was serving for the match. Djokovic did the same thing. They lost their serves while serving for the match. It happens to everybody.

What defines you as a player, and where you go as a player, comes down to how you're able to handle nerves. The people who are able to feel the situation, have an approach to that serve or a specific approach to that point, and have that fearless resolve are the players who will come out on top. You have to go out there, hit the right shot at the right time, and deal with those nerves.

Pete Sampras was the greatest player I ever played against. The reason he was great was his ability to play pressure points bigger than everybody else. It's as simple as that! And even he choked! I've seen matches where he gave up leads and didn't serve it out. It happens to everybody. Whether it's Michael Jordan, Tiger Woods, or Pete Sampras, you get out there and you deal with it. If you stumble, you pick up your hard hat, your work boots, and your lunch pail and you get right back to the task. Don't let nerves define who you are. Make sure you understand that if you're feeling nervous, the other side is feeling nervous too.

What does an athlete like Michael Jordan or Pete Sampras do differently than everyone else to handle those pressure moments so well?

It all comes down to a lot of preparation. They're talented, but there are a lot of talented players. However, there came a point—and I know this for a fact—where Sampras used pressure as a weapon. I always believed pressure was a weapon for me. Both sides feel the pressure, but I always believed I was going to be the one who used this weapon because I played better under pressure. I played better when I was on center court, when people were watching, and when I was on TV.

When more money was on the line, that was another weapon on my side, because I knew I was going to play better because of it. If you look at many elite athletes, that's what happens.

It's so close, and you've gotten to this point, this pivotal point of the contest where someone is going to lift their game, they're going to find another gear, they're going to find their execution. There's no doubt this is the way Sampras approached it. From first-hand knowledge that I gained by competing against him and watching him, he just got bigger and bolder and better as the pressure increased. Pressure can truly be a weapon! You can use it to benefit yourself, as a dagger, as a saber, or you can use it to tear yourself down. But you'll never use it to your advantage if you've convinced yourself you aren't a pressure player.

Pressure players lose. Pressure players double fault. Pressure players miss in big situations, but they're not afraid to take the same shot during the next point or at the next opportunity. They're fearless. There's no better place you want to be than when the match is on the line and everything comes down to your performance, and you come through! You've got to want that! If you don't want it, you'll always lose.

What's the secret to excelling at and enjoying practice?

I see a lot of burnout and a lot of progress being stalled because players stop looking for areas where they need to improve. They stay with their strengths. I see certain pros in the game of tennis, like Stosur at age 30-something winning her first US Open, or Schiavone at 30 winning the French Open. These are success stories because they kept on looking at parts of their game where they had to improve. They weren't done improving. You look at Tiger Woods changing his stroke after being the most dominant player in the world, or Nadal going from a clay-court player to an aggressive fast-court player on grass and hard courts by playing close to the baseline.

To me, you've got to have a plan. You need a short-term plan and a longer-term plan of where you want to be. For most players at 15 or 16 years old, if your plan is just to stay the same player you are, to just hit the ball a little bit harder, it's not going to be enjoyable. You're going to lose to the same player you've always lost to. You've got to have a big plan and a big picture, and you've got to understand that the process of getting better involves taking your time. It's not one big, bold step. It's a series of small, articulated steps that gets you better.

Can you describe the first time you played under the lights at the US Open?

I remember when I played at the US Open in '83; I threw up my ball toss and saw the Louie Armstrong stands. This was before Arthur Ashe Stadium was built. Normally as you go up to serve, you just see the blue sky and clouds, but because this stadium was so huge, the ball kept going up and I kept seeing stadium and more stadium. That's how I remember Louie Armstrong Stadium. It was on Court 7 in the old configuration. That court doesn't exist anymore. I was so thrilled and so excited to be out there, because this was really my life's work up to that point. I was 17 years old and I thought I'd lived a lifetime, but really, I hadn't done anything. I remember that my goal was to get to the US Open and to be a professional player. I was only playing the juniors in '83, but I'd accomplished a major step. I knew once I got there, I was going to make it as a pro.

Did you win?

I did, I did win!

What's the trick to juniors having a healthy tennis attitude on a consistent basis?

Everyone has to understand why they play the game. It doesn't matter if it's ALTA or if its juniors or peewees 10-and-under tennis, we all start playing the game because we enjoy it. We enjoy the game, and the more we play, the more we fall in love with the sport.

It changes everything when we start keeping score. Keeping score changes the dynamic altogether, and some people just can't handle losing. It hurts too much. No matter how hard you try, how hard you prepare, if losing truly takes the living heart out of you, if it takes away your spirit, your fight, and your passion for the sport, then it's going to be very tough.

The reality is that we lose a lot more than we win. If it's too hard to swallow that reality, then you're going to burn out and fade away. But if you truly love the sport and you truly enjoy playing, you're going to enjoy the process and you'll understand that losing is learning and that having setbacks makes you stronger. Being in those arenas where you're getting your tail kicked makes you better, if you approach it that way. Unfortunately, though, juniors often don't take ownership of their game. Mom and Dad drop them off, the pro feeds them a bunch of balls and tells them how great they are, what they need to do, and that's it. The player doesn't take ownership by saying, "Coach, this is where I need to get better. I get nervous on big points. I need to work on my volleys. I was at a tournament and my overhead let me down." I never hear that from a person who's just going through the motions. However, I do hear that from very passionate, very proactive players at all levels. They understand they need to get better, and losing reveals those areas of their game where they need work.

How do you transform a bad attitude into a good one... if that's possible?

Discipline. I don't think it's impossible. Most importantly, a coach and a parent have got to lay out the boundaries for that kid and that player. If that child doesn't want to live by those rules and play by those rules, you don't allow him or her to play and you don't spend the money to go out and do those things. They can play on the high school team or whatever.

I think it depends on the severity of the bad attitude. A parent can't be their child's friend. They've got to be the parent. Additionally, the coach can't be their friend, and it can't be a money situation. It's got to be a mentoring and leadership role. If the kid is throwing his racquet and losing his temper, you have to point-blank kick him off the court. If you don't do that, if you don't establish what constitutes a good attitude, what's right, and what's wrong, then you're going to lose them forever. They'll never reach their emotional and tennis potential.

How do you recommend young players keep a balanced life as they strive for collegiate or professional tennis careers?

The biggest thing is the word "no." The player must be able to tell their coach and their parents, "I really can't play today, I'm tired." The parents need to be able to read their child, and the coaches need to be able to read their student. They need to gauge if there are more "no" days than "yes" days, because that should be the test of the commitment from the parent and coach toward the talent. If the kid wants to go onto the court, then you're fine. If the kid is aching to get out there, that's great.

However, as soon as the kid starts saying "I'm too tired" or starts making excuses, then that's the Mendoza line.

The crucial test is at age 16, when the player gets their driver's license and has the option to either drive to practice or go hang out with her friends. When you look at the rankings of hot-shots that were ranked high in the 10's, 12's, and 14's, you'll see that at age 16, some of them just drop off the map. Tennis isn't what they want to do! The ones that dropped out were doing it because they were good at it. They weren't doing it because they were passionate about it and enjoyed it. That's the big difference between the people that go on and keep improving and developing in the sport, and the people who quit.

So, if they want this "tennis" lifestyle, a balanced life around tennis must be nurtured, or otherwise they'll most likely drop out?

Exactly! As a parent and as a coach, you've got to give the player structure and you've got to give them leadership. But the passion must come from the kid. You're wasting a lot of money, a lot of time, and a lot of energy if the kid truly doesn't show the passion for the game.

The biggest thing I've done in my six years at Syracuse is to take the kids who don't come to the court with the right mindset and the right energy and send them home. It's a privilege to be on the tennis court. I really stress that it's a privilege to play for me, and if I don't see the right attitude, you're not going to waste my time and you're not going to waste your time. The best thing I've done is to send kids home to work on their studies. They probably have something going on in their academic or social life and they just need some time away. They're not ready to give the 100% that I need from them. So, the more I keep them off the court, the more it keeps them in perspective. It's not a job. It's a place you come to enjoy your activity, your game, and this whole process.

Do you use many goal-setting practices with your players? If you do, what are your goal-setting methods?

Everything that we do is really based on competition. Everything we try to do in practice will have a winner and a loser. There's going to be an outcome. We try to put everybody in a pressure situation. I think pressure builds more confidence and creates more learning scenarios for the players. As far as goals, I only want Americans that want to play pro tennis. That's a big goal already. Concerning everything under that, we have fitness and strength goals, endurance and sprint goals, and other goals. Mostly all I want to see is that the players are a little bit better this week than they were last week. Sometimes it's tangible and sometimes it's not. Sometimes I'll test them. For example, let's put twenty serves in a row in the box. Who can do it first? We have competitions like that, because everything really revolves around competition.

What skills should a serious tennis player hope to gain, or take away, from a tennis-focused life?

Tennis really helps you understand yourself. As you grow up in the game, participating in an ongoing series of one-on-one conflicts, you recognize that it's really more of a conflict within yourself. The more you mature and understand how you deal with setbacks and adversity, the more it will make you stronger for the challenges that you'll face in your life. Tennis makes you have a little bit more courage and a little bit more self-confidence. When you're eventually on your own, this individual sport will benefit you. There's nothing more satisfying than putting in all the hard work and experiencing all those magical moments where it pays off. Tennis gives you another brick of confidence in your foundation that allows you to move forward with life.

Chuck Kriese :

Hall of Fame Coach
Author of Four Books on Tennis
Coach of Five Grand Slam Junior Titles

Chuck Kriese

Hall of Fame Coach, Author of Four Books on Tennis
Coach of Five Grand Slam Junior Titles

What pre-match rituals do you recommend for players to get their head in the right space before a match?

There are several things. I always recommend arriving at the court at least an hour ahead of time, preferably an hour and fifteen minutes ahead of time—never less than an hour. First, the player does the physical warm-up, then the mental warm-up, and finally the emotional warm-up. The players do thirty minutes of warm-up shots at the outset. Thirty minutes. Don't over-sharpen the knife. Just do enough warm-up so the player starts to sweat and his concentration is locked in. This has the added benefit of helping to deal with nerves.

Thirty minutes ahead of the start of the match, we go through a simple game plan about how the player wants to play. We focus on two or three things at the most, concentrating on the player's own game much more than on their opponent's game. The player needs to be the constant, and the opponent needs to be the variable. This is important. I think a lot of people make mistakes by trying to manipulate their game to fit into their opponent's game. I'm very big on getting my own player to focus on conquering their opponent's heart first and their head second. After that, the game will fall. I think most people make the mistake of trying to attack a person's game and play a certain style against that person. They usually change their game up, and that's a big mistake. You need to be the constant and your opponent the variable.

The two or three areas of focus during the mental warm-up are very simple things that fit into the player's strengths and how he wants to play. First, the player needs to lock into what he wants to do. Second, the player needs to upset what his opponent is trying to do. The important thing is to get locked in.

The last 15 to 20 minutes is all about being emotionally ready. The physical readiness has been accomplished by getting the sweat going, getting the tempo up, and getting the ball-striking up. Then the player does the mental part involving a simple routine to lock in how she's going to play. The last part is to try to get her butterflies to fly in formation. A player needs to feel pressure before going into play, but not too much pressure. The key with the emotional readiness in the last 15 to 20 minutes is to have a good balance of pressure. You never want the deer-in-the-headlights experience, where you're too nervous. You also never want the loosey-goosey attitude of, "I don't have anything to lose, so I'll just play loose." If you have that attitude, you always lose. You have to feel some pressure. You have to have butterflies, but they need to fly in formation.

To accomplish this balance, you put a few rituals in place. It's critically important to do these rituals on your own. You don't want to be around anybody else before you play. That's a very bad mistake. You need to be by yourself and complete your rituals. These could include stretching or jumping rope. Some people like to use a little music. Music is tricky, as you can have bad music (music that doesn't enhance your readiness) or good music. Rap or hip hop doesn't create the right frame of mind, but neither does classical music. You need more upbeat music to engage the right side of the brain, which is the creative side. I'm very big on country music or beach music or whatever engages the right side of the brain. It calms you.

So, all in all, the preparation is about an hour-long process. Take care of the physical, then the mental, and then the emotional part. If you do this successfully, when you hit the court, the controlled excitement and focus on being ready to play balances out the nervousness. The alertness you have when you hit the court has to be there. If I could describe it, it's like walking down a path through the woods and you know there are a lot of snakes. You've got to walk smoothly down the path, but you're very vigilant and focused. You notice everything. That's the way you need to be when you're ready to play.

Why does something like country music trigger the right, creative side of the brain and other music—let's say, rap—doesn't?

Rap music screws up your rhythm. On a competition day, you don't want your left brain to be in charge. Left-brain thinking is great for practice days. Right-brain thinking is better for game day. You basically need to be a detail-oriented person when you practice, but on game day, you need to be a riverboat gambler. Well, not necessarily a riverboat gambler, but the right side of your brain has to kick in. The creative side of your brain needs to be there. That's the secret Dr. Jim Pool gave me, and I completely agree.

Creativity is necessary to come up with strategies about how to win. Is that right?

No, no, no. The creative side of your brain allows your mind to work freely. You don't want your head filled with rigid guidelines during competitions, because all competitions are different. You train the same, 20 days in a row, but each competition is completely different. That's the beautiful thing about tennis. Tennis is more of an art form than a sports science. Because it's an art form, you want to use the creative side of your brain—the side that would play music or paint a picture or solve a problem. We always preach to kids, "You need a loud body but a quiet mind when you play." If your mind is loud and your body is quiet, you're going to lose.

Preparation is the key. The preparation ritual for a match is very individual and unique. It's usually through trial and error that players find the best routine for themselves. There's no cookie-cutter preparation formula except for getting the body ready, then the mind, and then the emotions. Take care of the body, then the head, then the heart. In a competition, it's all about prevailing over your opponent's heart first, his head second, and his game third.

I'm trying to understand this. By his game, you mean how he plays...

His strokes, his weaknesses, and his strengths. Most people try to think about this and analyze it. Most people try to dismantle somebody else's game by developing a strategy. The fallacy in trying to dismantle somebody's game before you're in the match is that in tennis, you're a batter first and a pitcher second. Most players regard themselves as a pitcher in that they try to deliver a ball a certain way. That player, as the batter, might not ever receive the ball that he's able to deliver in the way he intends. That's the problem. Good players don't allow you to hit the kind of balls you want to hit. The point is the best way to beat your opponent is to conquer their heart first. Conquer their heart then conquer their head, and the game falls.

It's not about the technical skills falling first, because everybody has had enough training and everybody's games are good. It's about making the person doubt what they're doing. Greg, you're aware of who Ernest Hemingway was, right. He used to say that all men have three battles in life: man versus man, man versus nature, and man versus inner man. To succeed in tennis, man versus inner man isn't an option. The minute you retreat into your inner man, you'll lose. However, the minute you can make your opponent retreat to his inner man, their game starts to unravel. Man versus nature is also not an option to be concerned about. Man versus nature might be bad line calls, referees, wind, rain—just bad breaks. The only thing for you to focus on—the way you need to focus when you play—is man versus man. You have to break your opponent's heart and overpower them mentally. You break their heart and get them to submit mentally. Once they fall into that space of being aware of their inner man and start worrying about their own game, the match is over quickly.

I'll tell you something. We had Mats Wilander come to our training center in College Park, Maryland about three times this year, He said something very profound: On practice day, everything is about your side of the court and trying to refine what you're doing. For this reason, you should want the toughest situation in order to have the best preparation. You should take care of the details. In other words, you're more melancholic, more detailed, and more left side of the brain on practice days. On game days, he said, it's all about your opponent. You become the constant and they're the variable. He's absolutely right. The minute you start worrying about your own game on game day, it's over. You saw Andy Murray at Wimbledon, when he lost in the final? There was a short period of time, in the third set, where he lapsed into his inner man, and that was the difference. It was completely the difference.

He started worrying about himself?

Yes.

I guess if you find yourself in that state of mind, you need to be prepared to break yourself out of it?

Yes. That's where the training comes in. Your training instills in you the belief that in everything you do, you remain the constant and your opponent is the variable.

This reminds me of when Del Potro beat Federer. His game was perfect. You know what I mean?

All players are going to lose sometime, like Nadal losing at Wimbledon. If you play Federer, Nadal, Djokovic, or even Murray, those players make you play at your 96th or 98th percentile to beat them. It's just the law of probability that nobody can do that very often, but now and then, someone does. Every player has their best game and every player has their worst game. The best players' worst game is very close to other players' best game. Del Potro is a good example. On a scale of 1 to 10, Federer's worst game is 8.5 and his best is 9.8. But you've got other guys whose worst game is 7 and their top game is a 9.5. That's the advantage. The reason the top guys keep winning isn't how good their top game is but how not-too-bad their bottom game is. That's the difference.

After a player loses a tough point, how do you recommend they get their mind back into focus?

It's interesting you ask that. I believe the rituals between points are critical. There are four ways you win or lose a point. These are: my good, my bad, your good, and your bad. That's it. If it's my bad or your good, of course, I lose the point. The obvious thing I've always done with players that I coach is make them acknowledge their opponent's good shot. They either clap the racket or say "Good shot" or nod their head and walk back. By acknowledging the other guy's good shot, you demonstrate a show of strength that keeps the pressure in balance.

For a player's own error, there's a particular ritual I have them do. I follow Jim Leahr's 15-second cure, because it's very good. I have my players turn around, walk back, and touch the fence. I have them say, "This (error) is good because..." and I make them finish the sentence. "This is good because it reminds me I've got to push off my outside leg, or, it makes me aware I was getting a little sloppy." They finish the sentence and see the lesson in the error. I tell them to say, "Do the next right thing" and to play to win.

When things happen, you either have a positive emotional response, a neutral emotional response, or a negative emotional response. When you win the point, you should feel a positive emotional response. Don't throw a party, but it's an emotionally good response, so you make a small fist or express it in some way.

Don't ever play bully tennis, by the way. I hate bully tennis. This is where a player yells, "Yeah, man, c'mon," and they get in the other person's face. That's crap. You don't do that. Some coaches teach that, but that's just crap. You express a positive emotional response when something good happens, but when you lose the point, you acknowledge your opponent's good play by clapping or saying, "Good shot." When you make a bad mistake, you say to yourself, "This is good because..." Then you touch the fence and remind yourself, "Play to win" or "Do the next right thing." These are both neutral responses, but they're essentially neutral positive responses. The wrong thing to do if you get upset or your opponent hits a good shot is to start thinking, "I'm playing badly." In a moment, you'll have lapsed into inner man.

Negative reactions are usually followed by a neutral response when you do something "bad". The best mindset is neutral; the worst is negative. Somebody who is completely out of control is usually a plus-minus. You need to be a plus-neutral with your responses. Jim Leahr's 15-second cure is probably the best thing out there as far as beneficial routines to do between points. His advice is about 30 years old—from the early '80s, I think—but it's still the best thing out there.

So you acknowledge that you have an emotion, then you think about what to do next, and then...

Do the next right thing. Yes, but hear me out. You don't control feelings. Feelings come and go. You control what you think about them and what you do about them. You do your best to control your body language, but sometimes you can't. Sometimes you get nervous, sometimes you don't. Sometimes you get anxious. Sometimes you rush. Emotions aren't controllable. What you think and do about them are controllable, and that's very critical. The benefit of routines is that they keep you locked into doing the next right thing. They calm you down. Routines calm

> "People who are great at what they do basically keep their eyes on the next five seconds."

you down or give you a focus. Maybe calm isn't the right word. Maybe it's better to say that routines give you a constant. They give you a constant before you play the next point.

If its match point and championship point; how do you keep yourself calm in that sort of elevated experience?

When your eyes look at the prize, they tell you many lies. My father used to say, "No matter what your aim in life, no matter what your goal is, keep your eye upon the donut, not upon the hole." He was basically saying, keep your eye on the process of what you're doing. Good players never look at the consequence of "this is a big point." They keep their focus. They know it's a big point, but they keep their focus on the process, never on the product. The process of what you're trying to do is what you need to focus on. Bad players, bad teams, and people that lose think too far ahead. People who are great at what they do basically keep their eyes on the next five seconds. You narrow your vision.

So you're saying you do your same ritual and come up with your game plan for just the next point, and whatever happens, happens?

Yes. It's not about how you win the point now, Greg. It's not about that. Your rituals are thoughts like, "I'm going to keep my feet aggressive," and "I'm going to go forward to meet the ball." Things like that. I always say a tennis match is like a cat. If you chase it and try to grab it, you're just focusing on the product. It runs away from you. Tennis should be called 'first you have, and then you don't.' You have no control over winning. You only have control over being a participant in the game.

Tennis is the toughest sport there is because there are only two gladiators in the arena. One must live, one must die. You might have a spear and the other guy's got a little pocket knife, but he can still kill you. If you're thinking about the product and what you get out of it, tennis will cut you up. It cuts you into bits. The point is, if you stay in the process, you have a better chance of winning. If you get into the product, you're dead.

What's the best way to bring out the inner confidence in a player?

Confidence is a combination of two things and two things only: Hard work followed by success. You earn your confidence through hard work. Repetition is the mother of skill. Basically, confidence comes through hard work and the belief that you own your game. You don't just rent your game. A lot of players don't do enough work and then, if they get a win, they easily go backwards. They don't gain confidence. You work hard, then you have success, and your confidence is locked in. If you work hard and don't win, it's a long process to gain that confidence. You've got to hang in there. But if you win and you don't work hard, you'll throw the game away just like easy money. You'll throw the win back. You don't go forward and climb. That's it. Confidence is built through hard work plus winning.

What's the most important thing to think about during a changeover?

When you have confidence, you go to your happy place, like Happy Gilmore. Actually, you shouldn't think about much at all. You shouldn't think about mechanics. Again, you don't go inner man. You clear the slate of your mind by using rituals and routines. That's why some players put towels over their heads. You narrow your eyes. You narrow your listening. You keep your eyes and your ears inside the tennis court. The routines are to get your breathing right and to get your mind calm. Again, this about keeping the right side of your brain engaged and not letting the left side take over. That's very critical.

The solution to a tennis match is always right in front of you. However, as the pressure mounts, players get frantic and they don't see the obvious. The solution is usually obvious. Once players get into to that deer-in-the-headlights place mentally, or there's too much pressure, everything becomes tedious. The simplest things start breaking down. So, to answer your question, you go to the sideline to balance your emotions, not to complicate your thoughts.

I just want to clarify what you said. You get out of the ritual process?

No, you don't get out. It's a different ritual. You have a ritual between points, because the game goes up and down, up and down, up and down. Then there's a little release of pressure when you go to the sidelines. You've got some time there. I've coached over 1,150 dual matches and also coached in college. Believe me when I say that most of the time, winning isn't about strategy. It's almost always about the winning player getting into emotional balance. Let me put it this way. In practice, you engage the body first and work on it. Then you mentally understand what you're trying to do. Then you get into balance emotionally. On competition days, the emotions have to be right in order for the thinking to be right and in order for the body to work properly. That's why I always say, "You break your opponent's heart first, her head second, and her game third."

Let's say a line judge makes a bad call and the player gets very emotionally off balance. Would this be a time for him to go to that Jim Leahr process?

You bet. Now, making a bad line call is man versus nature, and you don't focus on that. Bad line calls are just part of the game. I've taught many players over the years that if you get a bad line call, you just drop a ball, hit it backhanded, and say, "I shouldn't have missed that one." You know, it's just part of the game.

So you've just got to put that into your reality?

Yes. Listen, the game isn't set up to give you comfort. The game is set up to try to confuse you, puzzle you, and bring you every perplexing adversity possible. That's why you've got to keep a quiet mind and a loud body.

Let's say the match is getting pretty tight and the butterflies and nerves are getting pretty intense at this critical moment in the match. What's the best way to handle the pressure in this situation?

Every player knows what the right balance of emotional pressure is. Are you familiar with the Yates Inverted U Hypothesis? It's mentioned in almost every psychology book ever written. Sometimes it's called the pressure curve. Are you familiar with that?

No, sir.

It has an X-Y axis. One axis is performance and one is pressure. As pressure increases, performance increases until it reaches the apex of an inverted u. Once that place of maximum performance is reached, if the pressure continues to increase, performance cracks. Every player knows when he or she is ready and emotionally in balance. Every person is a little different in this regard. A really laid-back person might have to do a little bit more pumping up. The person who's already a little hyper does a little bit more calming down. There's a balance that you have to reach. There's a perfect emotional balance that each person has to get to.

You see Rafael Nadal out there jumping and dancing around. That's his deal. He does that to put a little fear into the other guy. The routines the players do all have that objective. Rafael Nadal picks at his underwear. Federer fixes his hair. They have rituals that they subconsciously do all the time. When they're doing those things, they're in the right emotional balance. Once a person passes the apex of that inverted u—it's called the Yates Inverted U Hypothesis—they'll perform poorly. That's why when people get ahead in matches, they sometimes play worse, and when they get behind, they often play better. When you're down, you play better because the pressure is on. You have to play better because you're backed into a corner. When you're ahead, you give yourself breathing room and you play worse.

In your opinion, what's the difference between the player who remains at around 50 to 100 in the world for most of their career and the player who's in the top 20 for most of their career? Considering everybody is talented, everybody works hard, what causes the difference?

The difference between the players who almost make it and the players that really make it is very simple. The players who most hate losing lose less. You only win to the level at which you can't stand losing. When players work hard; their hatred of losing increases. If players don't work hard, they'll let matches go. The bottom line is there are only two things involved: hating losing or loving winning. The hating losing is more powerful. It absolutely is. There are other things involved too. Some players are more clutch than others. They handle the pressure better.

It's really interesting to watch golf, isn't it? In golf, the pressure mounts, mounts, mounts, mounts, mounts. Only the players who've done the work and are ready to play carry the pressure. It's a really interesting scenario too. Almost 100% of the time, when I convince junior players to work a lot harder, they lose more matches for about a month because the pressure is greater. Then they grow into it and do better. You have to convince them to stay with the process during that month.

What's the trick for junior players to create and foster a healthy attitude on the tennis court on a consistent basis?

Very simple. It's summarized in the statement, "If you honor the game, the game will honor you." The game wasn't set up for your comfort. It wasn't set up for your advancement in life. The game is way bigger than any individual player in it. If you have the attitude of honoring the game and respecting all opponents, you'll never get in your own way. The minute you start thinking that tennis is there to serve you, you're going to have some nasty, tough experiences and a lot of pain because this game will cut your heart out and stomp on it. But if you honor it, it will honor you.

Let's say you have a player you're coaching and she has a bad attitude. Would you say exactly what you just said to me to transform her thinking, and has that been effective?

I say that probably twice a day to kids. If a player has a bad attitude, that means they're self-centered. That's really what a bad attitude is: self-centeredness. There are two kinds of people. People that think about themselves and people that think about other people. The bottom line is that a bad attitude can come in a lot of different forms.

If a person is competitive, they're sometimes thought to have a bad attitude, but that may not be the case. Attitude determines your altitude, they say. There are all these little clichés you can repeat, but in the end, it comes down to disrespect for this wonderful game and a player putting himself on a higher pedestal than the game. The minute you try to approach this game with the perspective of, "I'm going to advance myself and beat somebody else," you're in for a long one. If you approach it with, "I'm a competitor and I'm honored to be on this playing field against this other competitor. I have to honor the game," then you're in business. When that's your attitude, your mind works right, you solve problems, and you look at the competitive situation in the right way. If a pianist or a musician doesn't respect the music, that's shameful. If a tennis player doesn't honor the game of tennis, that's shameful. It's just flat-out wrong and shameful. Once a player believes that he's participating in something that's bigger than himself, he plays with a completely different mentality.

How do you recommend young players keep a balanced life but still have the appropriate emphasis on tennis to keep their professional dreams alive?

The key is keeping a balanced life. I like people to learn how to develop a maximum passion for something. I'm not big into having plan Bs when it comes to life. I think the mistake we make, especially in the United States, is everybody thinks they have to have a plan B, a plan C, and a plan D. Tennis is a passionate activity, a passionate affair of the heart. If a person wants to become a true participant in the game of tennis, her heart must be engaged. You could play tennis every day of your life for six hours a day and never be a tennis player. You could go to school every day of your life and never be a student. You could play music every day of your life and never be a musician. You have to engage your heart. The other areas of life that need to be kept balanced are hobbies and such, but tennis must be their passion activity.

I used to tell my kids that they have three times during their day. They have their dirty-work time, where they have to take care of things they've got to do. They have their passion time, and they have their free time. Tennis shouldn't be dirty-work time. It should be passion time. You protect it, you honor it, and you have an inquisitive mind to try to learn everything you can about it. Your free time is different than this. You have to be in love with tennis. You're a well-rounded person in many things because you've learned how to give your heart to one thing. If you don't learn how to give your heart to one thing deeply, you're going to be pretty mediocre at everything. The only thing you'll be good at is being mediocre.

What's the dirty work? What does that mean?

Dirty work involves things like getting your running in, brushing your teeth, and carrying out the garbage. You have to eat well, sleep well, get your equipment right, string your rackets, and do your preparation work. Those are all dirty work. The tennis itself is about having passion. You know, it's funny. When kids go on to the court, I'll remind them of the movie "Gladiator" and say, "What did Maximus do every time he got ready for a battle?" He'd get down, grab a handful of soil, and rub it between his hands. Sometimes I get the kids to do that when they go out onto the tennis court.

Have you ever thought about how bad we are at honoring the tennis court? You know, that battlefield? Kids will throw wrappers around and have banana peels lying around. Here's a beautiful thing: In '09, I was coaching the Thai kids for the Southeast Asia Tennis Federation. A couple of our players got to hit with Nadal. He was a 17-year-old kid and Nadal is hitting with him and there are probably three thousand people watching Nadal practice. Right after they finished, Nadal goes over, grabs the broom, sweeps his own court, and does the lines. He also picked up every wrapper, every turner grip, and all the trash around his chairs. It wasn't Uncle Tony who did it. Nadal did it all. It was a beautiful thing that showed honor for the game. That's the deal. That's what it's about. I can't emphasize this enough. Once the kids understand this, then it becomes a whole different endeavor and they see each tree in the forest. They see all the little things they're blind to when they look at tennis as a self-serving endeavor.

As opposed to something that they are privileged to be a part of?

Yes. It's about honor. Each of us has a family. My father used to say, "Never bring shame on the family name." The minute you go onto that tennis court, you never bring shame on the game of tennis. You honor it. If you honor it, it will honor you.

That's a good example. Are you a really firm believer that your career must be passion-filled work?

Of course. We can either have a vocation or an occupation. Teaching and coaching is a vocation, and I'm going to keep working as long as I can in this because, at the bottom of my heart, I know this is the gift that God has given me and this is what I'm supposed to do with my life. It comes down to a service in which you help other people. Have you ever heard of the law of reciprocities? Whatever you give to others, you get back ten-fold. It's a law of nature and the law of the universe. If you hoard things, you become poorer. If you give things away, you become richer. I'm not into giving things to people who haven't worked for anything or people who are lazy. I'm very, very stingy with my time if the student isn't trying. Every coach knows this, if they've been around for a while. If the student isn't trying, you do window-dressing coaching. You don't go deep enough to where you open up your heart. Once you believe the student is good, you open up your heart. Then it becomes a long affair of the heart where you give everything. There's no motion without emotion. Nothing happens until you get the student to engage his heart.

Do you use many goal-setting practices with your players? If so, what are they?

There are "process' goals and there are "product" goals. The product goals are what you want to try to accomplish. I think there are two things you need to know to really improve. You need to know where you're trying to go, but you need to know where you're at, too. Most players will say, "Hey, I want to win, I want to be ranked such and such," but they don't really know where they are with their game. Everybody judges themselves as better than they really are or higher than they really are. I'm much more into process goals—how you go about everything and how you go after everything. You don't dumb down what you try to go after. Hear me out on this. The goal is to be ranked number one in the world at being yourself. If you're ranked 1000th in the world at tennis and you're 100% who you really are, only you can judge the value of that as you put your head down at night. Tennis takes a lot of things. It takes the ability to desire opportunity. It takes God-given ability. It takes the opportunities that parents, coaches, and teachers provide. The desire of the individual has to be a pure motive. It's not just about being someone who tries hard. It has to be a pure motive.

Again, a mistake is made when people try to get something out of tennis instead of honoring it. Goals, when you write them down, start to become magic. It's really interesting how that works. My wife and I have a sort of wish list at our home. We wrote down eleven goals, and seven years later we'd accomplished nine out of the eleven. We'd hardly looked at them in those seven years. A goal isn't something as stupid as, "I'm going to be number one in the world." It needs to be specific, such as, "I want to be on the ATP tour by such and such a date." You pursue things at that level. I'm not in favor at all of saying, "Well, I'm just going to do the best I can." That's a complete cop-out. When you write goals down, they should be like the desktop icons on your computer screen. They're right there in front of you all the time. If you don't write them down, they basically become like something that's buried in your computer. You have to look through 18 files and then you still can't find it. It's got to be right in front of you all the time. But again, it can't be, "I've got to be number one in the world." You have to know where you're trying to go, where you're at, and how you get there. And it must be a passionate journey of the heart.

You don't have your kids reviewing their goals every month or week or anything like that?

No. I used to review goals once a year and let the kids know it. This worked best when the kids wrote down their goals on two pieces of paper and I put one in my office in an envelope. I'd have them write down short-term, medium-term, and long-term goals—one for three months out, one for a year out, and one for four years away. It was amazing. If they wrote down their goals, they almost always accomplished them. I didn't harp on them once they wrote them down. It's like saying, "I'm going to drive to St. Louis." Once you say, "I'm going to drive to St. Louis," you don't have to ask, "Where are we going? When are we going to St. Louis? Did you forget? We're in Memphis now. Oh, okay. We're going to go to St. Louis." You don't have to do that. Once you decide what level you're going after, you don't have to keep saying it. What needs to be emphasized repeatedly is the process. "I need to do a little more of this" or "I need to do a bit more of that. I need to do more running. I need to do more ball-striking drills. I need to do..." You redo the process goals, but the product goals of deciding what you want out of something are only done once.

What's your method for helping junior players overcome those moments of burn-out?

I don't believe in burn-out. You never hear someone who's winning a lot say, "I'm burned out," do you?

No.

It's sort of like the guy who catches the touchdown pass in the end zone and gets nailed by three people. He jumps up and runs off the field. But the guy who drops the ball sort of limps off, right? It's the same thing with burn-out. I've coached for forty straight years now and I've never felt burned out. You basically have to change the way you go about things. You're constantly learning. You have to keep interested. You have to keep changing it up a little bit. I try to stay old-school without being old-fashioned, if you know what I mean. There's no burn-out. That's a real cute statement that some administrator came up with who thinks the kids are working too hard. Now, there's a staleness that happens when people train without a purpose. If you train without a purpose, you will get bored. The key in coaching is to come up with ways to keep people going.

Let me give you an example. We're having a really crummy day with maybe 20-mile-an-hour wind. It's cold and nobody wants to be there. On those kinds of days, I tell the players, "Okay, your goal today is to win 100 points. Go get it done." You give them a mission, something to accomplish. You have to have some kind of mission for people to keep their mind off the repetitive tasks. Look at it this way. You play tennis, so didn't you ever imagine yourself playing Arthur Ashe or Borg or somebody as you were hitting on the backboard when you were a kid? I used to play Dennis Ralston or Arthur Ashe when I was a kid on the backboard. I used to make games up. I'd visualize myself playing these guys. I mean, come on, hitting on the backboard is about the most boring game there is. But if you use your imagination, your mind goes to a place where you can still initiate the passion.

When players are on losing streaks, they begin to say that they're burned out, they need to rest. No, they don't. They need to get a couple of wins under their belt to get out over the hump. This is an absolute truth in tennis: Right before players make a jump, they always have a real hard time winning. There's a saying: "Breakdowns happen before breakthroughs."

The breakdown happens to test your will to go forward. The game humbles you before it lets you go forward.

What skills should the serious tennis player hope to gain and take away from living a tennis-focused life?

Oh gosh! Do you want a whole encyclopedia? I mean, c'mon. Where do we start? Work ethic. Life isn't fair. Life isn't equal—we only have equity; we don't have equality. Honesty. Dealing with adversity. Embracing adversity. Compassion for the person you beat. Humility when you win. Conditioning. Strength of mind, body, and spirit. Through your training, you create a resource within yourself—like digging a well—that's filled with all the good things in human nature. This resource will help you get through the rest of your life. You learn to compete. Being a competitor is a lot different than just being someone who tries hard. Being someone who only tries hard is the ultimate cop-out. You have to compete in every competition. You learn to not rationalize. You learn to not make excuses.

What's the difference between someone who tries hard and someone who's a competitor?

What do you think it is? Now c'mon, think about it. Those who try hard say, "I'm doing my best." Competitors say, "I'm fighting." Like I told you earlier, the difference between the people who make it and those who don't is that the people who make it hate losing more. Competing is competing. If you match it up head to head, toe to toe, like two boxers in a boxing match, there's nowhere to go. Whether you're in the ring or on the tennis court, you have to look the other person square in the eyes and say, "I will not break. I'm going to make you break." Someone who tries hard says, "Oh, I did my best. I ran hard, I tried hard, I sweated hard."

Tennis humbles you. Realizing that life isn't fair, free or equal is a great lesson of tennis. Cheaters win sometimes. You might train forever and then crazy things happen. You have no control over winning or losing. You only have control over your effort. If you haven't paid the price and given your heart, you won't reap any benefits in the long run. You're only promised equity, which means an equal chance. There's no equality. One person has a bigger serve, one person has more opportunity. One person has this, one person has that. But equity is the important thing that people learn.

Here's the deal. In the end, you have control over what you have control over. Tennis is an objective sport. It's not like art or music where you have a judge judging you. If you're good enough, you can advance. If you're not good enough, you don't advance. Think about being a pro tennis player. You could turn pro tomorrow or I could turn pro tomorrow. We could have a ten-year-old kid turn pro tomorrow. We have these US TA qualifying tournaments where you have 50 people competing. If they win, they could go to the qualifying US Open and if this guy here wins 15 straight matches, he's going to be a world hero. That's the beautiful thing about tournament sports. All you have to do is be good enough. I always tell the kids, "Don't work to get a pedigree, work to get better." Everybody in tennis wants a pedigree. They want a starting place. They like to start on third base, with either better equipment or better opportunities or playing in a tournament that's better. In the end, you should only want to have a higher skill level. Remember, if you honor the game, the game will honor you.

Bruce Levine:

Former professional tennis player and coach of both professional men and women tennis players

Bruce Levine

*Former professional tennis player and coach of both
professional men and women tennis players*

**Can you tell me about the pre-match rituals you recommend
to help players get their head in the right mindset before a
big match?**

I'm a big believer in rituals, which I begin the day before
a match. I do a number of different things with my players to get
them ready. We discuss nutrition and talk about their habits. I'm
also a big believer in visualization. Some of the kids that I coach
watch their favorite players on a video the day before the game.
We sometimes prepare like that, where they sit and watch, mentally go through the motions, and visualize themselves playing
their opponent. In the warm-up with me or with another player (that isn't their opponent), there's a ritual we do where they
play for twenty-five to thirty minutes, an hour or two before the
match. It could be mini-tennis leading up to some point play,
just to get their blood flowing. Some of the kids like music,
so to get in the groove, they'll sit down in a corner and put on
their iPod.

There's always a conversation about how we're going
to play the match that day—what we want to look for on the
other side of the net and what we want to do on our side of the
net. Plan A and Plan B. So, if I have a kid that has a two o'clock
match, at 7 am that day I'll be working on that player in my
head, and I'm on that kid by ten o'clock in the morning.

What do you mean when you say "You're on that kid?"

After we have breakfast, we turn on a video of their favorite players. I want them watching those players play a dozen points so that they can visualize themselves in those positions. Then we do a warm-up and talk about how they are going to play the match and their overall game-plan. Then if they want to sit in the corner and listen to music, that's the time to do it. Then they're ready to play.

All right, let's say it's match point and championship point. How does a player keep herself calm and focused?

I'm a big believer in breathing. I want to see a player take a lot of deep breaths before the point starts, not to hyperventilate though. Also, in the pre-match, I'm going to talk to her about this being the moment she's been waiting for—this is the place. If she's been hitting a forehand crosscourt or a backhand crosscourt throughout the match, maybe, for this point, she should do a serve and volley. For one thing, it's going to force her to stay focused because it's a little bit different from what she's been doing. Secondly, it's going to shock her opponent a little. The opponent won't be expecting it. Change it up!

Some players love that, but others are like, "Nah, I'm not doing that. It's like going out of the realm a little bit." With the player that says, "No, I'm not gonna do that," I'm going to tell him or her that I want them to play a steady point, focus on the target areas—where they want to hit the ball—and play the point. I tell them not to worry about their opponent. Play their point and breathe. Breathe, breathe, and breathe. That helps to get rid of some of the nerves and keep doing what has worked.

So, beforehand, just breathe, and think about the strategy?

Yes. I tell them to play out the point in their head. There are guys and girls that I work with who will play 85% of the match from the baseline. They come to match point and they're like, "Okay, I'm going to serve and volley here." I can live with that and then the breathing settles the nerves.

Do you have people play out, in their head, every point? Or how many points per match do you have the person play out in their head?

Well, I think you have to play the big points out in your head because those points are the points where you're going to get tight and you're going to feel uncomfortable and under pressure. In general, I like the players to think about how they want to play each point, but it's cumbersome for the player to say to himself, "Okay, I'm going to play every point out in my head." A match would take a month. Basically, I think each player should stick to their general game plan for the majority of the match but on the big points they should have a more detailed strategy.

The big difference between each level of player is how they can stay really focused throughout the whole point. It seems that once the focus dissolves, they typically lose the point. So, what do you think is the trick for a player to stay in the zone consistently?

I think the player that stays focused throughout the point is somebody who's already intense and has strong habits. He watches the ball and doesn't worry about anything else. He'll watch the ball, play the ball, and hit almost every ball perfectly. A focused player pays attention to her movement while she's out there playing. She doesn't think about what her opponent is doing. I think if you were to ask Rafa or any of the guys at that level, "What are you doing?" they'd say they're not worried about the other guy. They'd say they're only concerned about what they're doing. They're focused on hitting their shot. I think that's what keeps them in the zone. I think they know what their opponent likes to do and they might know their pattern or where they like to play the ball, but Nadal isn't focused on Federer. Nadal is focused on Nadal. He's thinking, "I'm going to hit this ball. I'm going to hit that ball."

It's just a ball coming at him. It doesn't matter who's on the other side?

Correct.

One of the big differences among players, at any level, is the degree of confidence. How do you take a kid that's talented but doesn't have a high confidence level and bring out that inner confidence in them?

I think the key is the level you play them, how you play them, and how you bring them along. My strategy is that I want each kid to play where they win some match from the get-go and if possible get them matches that are competitive. I want their matches to be very close and very tight, even though that might not be what the parents want. I get involved in making the decisions about where to play the kid, and the parents don't always agree with me. I explain to them, that I'm going to teach their child how to win, and with wins comes confidence. If you look though tennis history, you see this. Lendl was just a good player until he beat McEnroe and then all of a sudden no one could beat him; same thing with Nadal and Federer. Winning is the number-one confidence builder.

Number two is complimenting hard work. I talk to the kids all the time about how hard they work. I say, "Okay, you spent two hours on the court today. You can wring your shirt out. You worked really hard. You worked well. You didn't just go out and play around. You went out and put your nose to the grindstone. You worked hard. You hit 50 forehands, 50 backhands in a row. You served 200 balls. You served and volleyed 80 times. You deserve to feel confident about the work that you've done, and you need to carry that confidence with you onto the court."

The other thing I say to the kids all the time is, "When you play, it isn't going to matter whether you win or lose. Your parents aren't going to stop feeding you and I'm not going to stop coaching you. You're not going to go without shoes. So, go play." The problem isn't with the body; it's with the mind. The body can do it but the brain doesn't let the body flow. I let the kids know there's no downside to hitting the ball. There's no downside to going for it, provided what they do is smart shot making and selection. This encouragement gives them the freedom to start to feel confidence in their ability to say, "Okay, it doesn't matter. I'm going to go for the shot." With the correct mechanics and training, those shots start to become successful. That, in turn, builds confidence.

The hard work brings you the wins, then the wins give you the results, and the results give you the confidence?

Right. But I really think you have to have kids playing at the right level first. This is critical. Also, it does not come 1, 2, 3; it takes work.

What's the most important thing for a player to think about during a changeover?

I want the player to think first of all about breathing and relaxing as much as possible during those 90 seconds. The second thing I want him to think about is where he is, what's going on, and if anything has changed. He needs to be aware if his opponent has started to do something that he needs to take note of. If so, he needs to think about altering his game—to defend, or to get offensive again, or vice versa. Those are the big things. If there are any mechanical issues, this is the place for the player to take a couple of seconds and tell herself, "Maybe I'm hitting my forehand a little bit late. Let's get out on it a little bit sooner." It's about the big picture.

Butterflies and nerves have the ability to be a positive force, if channeled correctly. How do you help your players learn how to channel their butterflies positively?

The only thing I can say about that is that everybody gets butterflies. There's an optimal level of excitement that sports psychologists talk about. They'll tell you that you don't want to have too much but you want to have enough. You want to be on edge but you don't want to have bloodshot eyes and adrenaline flowing through your veins at 95 miles an hour. It's tough, but yes, I want the players to have those nerves. I'm glad they're nervous. I'm glad they have that edge, because they can use that edge to help them focus and keep moving. I also encourage players to "whack a few" during the warm up.

Movement can channel your butterflies, help you get off your feet, and pump you up, correct?

Yes, but I see too many people come out overexcited and they kill all their gas too quickly. They use all their fuel, and before they know it, they're down in the dumps. Not only are there no more butterflies, there's no more excitement. An opponent can just roll over a person like that.

In a situation where you lose a point due to something out of your control, like the line judge making a bad call, how do you recommend getting yourself back into the game?

In that type of situation, I say to a player, "What I want you to try to do, with all your might, is play comfortably and win the next point. In addition, to get yourself back into it, I want you to turn around, face the back curtain or the back of the court, and take a deep breath. Close your eyes, find your happy place, and then turn back around and energize yourself." Obviously you can't forget it all, but you can go back to the adage of "Don't let one point cost you five." A bad call is out of your control. There's nothing you can do about it. Don't take it home. Just leave it there. It's done. By all means, talk to the judge. Vent if you need to, within your rights and within reason, but after you've done that, it's gone, you can't turn the clock back.

Obviously, the judge in the chair isn't going to change anything, so gather yourself up by taking a deep breath, facing the other way, and then turn back around with a fresh start. First, let it go verbally. Talk to the official and say, "Are you really sure? Did you see it that way?", then, after you've spoken your peace, go back and start again. Let's go!

Just thinking about what we talked about, maybe visualization would be a good idea there.

This would be an excellent place for a player to visualize playing the next point. It's a way of saying, "Okay, it's gone. Let's visualize what's coming next."

What, in your opinion, is the difference between a player that stays ranked 50 to 100 in the world throughout their career and one that's in the top 20 to 30 for most of their career? Since everybody is typically talented and everybody works hard, what's the big difference?

Confidence and mental acuity. I know about this from my friend, Mr. Lendl. I remember very clearly being in Madison Square Garden, watching him play Andre Agassi. He was down a bit in the match, but his attitude and look was, no worries I can pull this off. And he did. By the same token, I saw him play in Dallas at the WTC Championships and watched him play McEnroe. He hit McEnroe with a ball and McEnroe's attitude drastically changed. I remember seeing the look of "uh-oh" on Ivan's face and McEnroe got very serious and focused. The disparity of talent between the number one ranked player and the number 20 ranked player isn't very big. However, those guys that are in the top five, they're winning sets in the locker room before they even walk onto the court.

Look back at Steffi Graf. I remember being with a player I was coaching on the women's tour. She walked into the locker room and said, "Oh man, I've got to play Steffi Graf." "Yes, and she's human, like you," I said. "But its Steffi Graf," she said. So I said, "You're screwed, pardon my French. You want to bow down or you want to play? Those players have an aura about them and I think, in the back of their mind, they're saying,

'No one is getting me unless I get myself.' You have to believe that you can go out and beat most of these people. Having said that, everyone has days where they're vulnerable, whether it's because they're tired or they're just not feeling 100%.

I agree. One of the things that motivated this book was my experience volunteering at the Atlanta Tennis Championships (Professional Tennis Tournament). I was around the players throughout the week, and I remember seeing them and thinking, "No one is really that much bigger than me and they don't appear to be that much stronger." So, I began to think, "Why couldn't I have done this?" There's no reason that I couldn't.

Actually, there is a reason. Some of those guys are much tougher mentally than most of the people you or I will ever meet. The amount of work these players put in is astounding, and yet some people begrudge them the money they make. Again I'll say that with hard work comes a sense of, "Okay, I've done this. I've earned this."

I do all the racket reviews for Tennis Magazine and Tennis.com. If somebody asks me about a racket, of course I can talk about that racket. However, I work with a 24-year old writer, and if you ask him about rackets, he may have doubts about some of them. The difference between me and him is that I've seen enough and done enough that I'm more knowledgeable, more prepared, and more confident and comfortable with the topic and material.

Desire—that's the difference?

The desire is there, I think, in most players. You reach a

point in a match when it's hot and it's humid and you've been out there for two hours and you're thinking to yourself, "So, do I really want this? Man, I could go jump in the pool if I lose this point. If this guy plays a good point, I'm in the water and it's cool or I'm back in the hotel with the A/C on." There are a million and one things you could be doing but you have to believe you can win. You have to have the desire to win but you also have to have the confidence. I think the ultimate word is confidence. The top players reach a point where they don't believe they can lose. The players that are ranked 50-100 and below doubt they can win, more often than the top 10-20.

What's the secret to excelling in and enjoying practice?

Practice has to be fun as well as hard work. You have to do things besides just tennis. We used to play a lot of soccer with the tennis ball. We also used to play football and basketball. With some players we do a lot of cycling on the road, aerobics... So, number one, practice isn't just tennis.

Number two, you have to be willing to let your player, or players, have some fun, simply because it is hard work. Take a player who's thinking, "I'm going out on the court for four hours and I have a list of things I need to accomplish." On that list is A, B, C, and D, and they all suck. To me, that's not fun at all. You've got to hit 80 forehands in a row because you're still having trouble or the balls have got to be deeper. This sort of practice can be pretty boring. So I encourage players to make a game out of it. If you have somebody who's hitting with one of your players, include pushups and sit-ups. Let me tell you, I used to have a washboard stomach because I didn't win!

What's the trick for junior players to create and foster a healthy tennis attitude on a consistent basis?

There are a couple of things. The first one is, as a coach, you can't treat the players like anything other than a person. Yes, they're tennis players, but they're also human. When you travel—and I spent a lot of time traveling—we go to the movies and we go out to dinner. We do normal stuff. I make things stay normal. The players must spend time with their family. I try to keep life as normal as possible. The players have to focus on their tennis, but tennis should be regarded as a job by these young adults. Their attitude is, "This is work and everybody our age goes to work." So they look at it like work. Their hours might be a little wacky but this is their job. Their job is to be in good shape, hit the ball well, and stay in tune with everything that's going on. Outside of work, I want them to live as normal a life as possible. Yes, they travel more. Yes, people might notice them more or they might be a more visible name or person, but they still need to have a normal social life and family life as much as possible. So I emphasize including lots of normal stuff.

With a high-school kid, school keeps a kid somewhat regular. When a parent says to me, "We're going to take the kid out and home school him," I want to ask them why. Keep them in school or, if you send them to an academy, they go to school at the academy and are required to keep their grades up. They're required to do obligatory family things like visit grandma and grandpa and so on, to keep life as normal as possible. As a coach of high school kids, the first question out of my mouth every day is, "How was school, guys? What did you do in school today?" The answer I always get is, "Nothing," but at least they know I'm not saying, "Screw school; we're just worried about your forehand."

I have a pact with all the players that I coach. I'm not coaching that much anymore because I run a club, but what I say to my players the first time I'm around them is, "When you come out to practice and your girlfriend broke up with you or you flunked a test, I want you to tell me about it because when I start to push your buttons (and I'm not always the nicest guy walking the streets), I don't want you to turn around and tell me to go take a hike. If you do, I'm going to hit you." Not physically, but I'm going to give you a hard time. You don't tell me to take a hike—I'm the boss. But, if you tell me, "My girlfriend dumped me in fourth period today and I've been moping around ever since," I might have a little sympathy for you and I might try to talk to you about it so that you can get it out of your system a little.

What's the secret to transforming a player's bad attitude into a positive one?

My main job as a coach, in terms of talking to a player, is about keeping the perspective that the glass is half full versus half empty. The other thing I do sometimes with players is chart them. I draw a horizontal line across the middle of the page. If they win a point, I make a mark above the line. If they lose a point, I make a mark below the line. When there are more marks below the center of the page than above it, I say, "Here's a ditch. You're fighting to get up and out of the ditch." And I use the power-word system because I love that thing. I think it works very well. In addition, this chart exercise can be more detailed for sure and with all the apps out today much more technical. The big thing is that is shows trends.

Anything else?

I try to get them involved so they can get rid of the bad vibes as much as possible. I also talk to them. I say, "So, you lost the point. If your opponent played well, I want you to give your opponent the credit. You don't have to bow down and kiss his knee, but you have to tell him "good shot," because that validates your loss of the point. It also lets your psyche know you give credit where credit is due and you didn't screw up. That guy did a good job and you're acknowledging it. You've got to be able to give your opponent credit where credit's due. That's number one.

Number two is, when you make a mistake, you can't take it back. There's no turning the clock around. Having a bad attitude about it is only going to hurt you more and more. So, you need to start to think positively about things and say, "Okay, here's what I did well." When kids make mistakes and I hear them say, "I suck," I get upset. What they should be saying is, "I tried the shot and it didn't work. Next time, I want to try something else." Again, try to turn the internal conversation that we all have with ourselves into a positive conversation. Repeating to yourself, "My footwork stunk today" or "my forehand stunk" isn't going to get anybody anywhere.

What should a player say to herself when she's playing poorly and needs to turn her game and attitude around?

You say, "I'm trying to hit this forehand hard today. I want to make sure I get out on the ball early next time." Instead of saying, "That forehand stunk" and walking away, she says, "I missed that forehand because I hit it late. I want to take it earlier. I want to get my feet into a better position before I release on the ball." You want to tell yourself those kinds of things. One of the things everybody knows about me is I can find a problem in anything. In every email I send about a problem, I say "I'm willing to help try to solve the problem because I'm not going to just ditch it without trying to be a part of the solution." I have time limitations in life, but I say, "Here's the deal, here's the problem. What can I do to help you fix the problem?" I want my kids to think the same way. If you have a problem, how are you going to fix this problem? It's not a problem that's going to blow up the Earth. It's a problem with your forehand! How are you going to fix it and how are you going to get your psyche to be comfortable with you? Figure it out.

So talking positively is always the best way to go, and this is a matter of training. When you're in a practice match situation and you're down on the court with a player, you listen to what the player says. You go over there, you grab him by the shirt, and you say "Whoa! Don't tell yourself you stink. Even if you don't believe it, if you say it often enough, you're going to start to convince yourself. You then need to tell yourself, "You know what? I don't stink; I just missed the forehand because my feet weren't in the right place. I've got to get my feet there."

Do you use many goal-setting practices with your players and, if so, what do you recommend?

Yes, I do. When I first start coaching a player, I give them an index card and say, "Here is where you are. Where do you want to be in three months, six months, nine months and twelve months? I want some answers." It's not like, "Yeah, I want to be better and my mother wants me to be better too." I want that player to tell me where they think they belong in terms of their ranking. What about their strokes? Do they want to change and why? What do they want to add to their game and what do they want to get rid of in their game?

Any time one of the players gives me some attitude, I go and get the index card. "Okay, you told me you want to be here. Guess what? Here are the steps you need to take to get there. Right? Didn't we have this conversation? So, how come you're not following the path we discussed?"

Do you write down those things you talk about?

Yes, on the index card.

You write down the steps?

The first time, I write down the goals. The second time, we sit down and I say, "It's okay. I've seen you hit the ball and I understand what you want to do. Now tell me what you think you need to do to accomplish these goals". I ask the player to do that, and I do it myself. Then we come to some sort of an agreement.

I always use my large belly as an example. I have a belly and I want to lose weight. Here are my options: I can eat lots of salad and I can see a nutritionist. If I eat a lot of salad and I see a nutritionist and he tells me to eat chicken and turkey breasts and no more hamburgers and I go to McDonalds, who do I have to blame? I can't look at the nutritionist and say, "What are you doing?" He told me what to do; I've got to execute it. I'm the player.

The other thing that I want my players to ask themselves and me is, "Why am I doing something?" If I'm making them hit forehand volleys down the line instead of cross court, I want the player to ask himself why am I making him hit them down the line or why am I changing his grip or why is my footwork a little different or why did I hit that ball with a closed stance? I want those questions because I want to open that dialogue up and I want the lines of communication to be as free and clear as humanly possible. I want them to know that I respect their thoughts and opinions, and I want them to have the same feeling towards me.

How do you push your players when they don't feel like training or when they get burned out?

Sometimes, when kids are burned out, you've just got to tell them to go home. I used to work with this kid who played at the college level. He was a really nice kid and a hard worker. His parents were a little overzealous. We went on a four- or five-tournament run together. By the time we got to the last of the five tournaments, this kid just broke down and cried. Sixteen-year-old kids don't do that, normally. He told me, "I don't want to be here. I've had enough." You need to know, even in a practice situation, when it's time to take a day off. Sometimes taking the day off to be with your friends is the best thing in the world.

Sometimes kids are just lazy. So I show them their card. "Hold on a minute. I'm going to my office. Here's your index card, Jack. What's the story? You want this? Well, here's what you have to do to get this. We both agreed on this. Let's go. If you need a day off, you need to tell me. Don't take a day off out of the blue. Come to me and say, "My girlfriend dumped me. I need a day of mourning". Or, "I was out till two o'clock last night drinking. I'm sorry, but I need to take the morning off." In which case, I'm probably going to tell him to go run the lake in 90-degree weather. Don't do that again! *[Laughs]*

You want them to take some time off when they're burned out, but not slack off when they just want to be lazy?

Right. I don't want a slacker. However, I think part of the responsibility lies on my shoulders to see that Johnny needs a day off or Johnny needs a light practice today. Here's something that cracks me up. The women, more so than the guys, are afraid to take a day off. It's like they're going to forget how to play. What? Do you forget how to eat? No. You don't eat everything, all day, every day.

What skills should the serious tennis player hope to gain and take away from living a tennis-focused life?

Tennis is a very, very good symbol for life. There's a lot of similarity or symmetry in tennis that applies to life. You may get into a tough situation on the tennis court and you have to figure out what to do—to fight hard, be steady, and say, "I'm not going to get too aggressive." There are other situations on the tennis court where you have to be really aggressive, whether you want to be or not. The player must be able to say to herself, "I have to fight hard. I have to be willing to endure." This is what life is about. I could tell you some of the stuff that went down in my life and you would think, "No, really?"

Tennis has been a great metaphor for me my whole life. I was recently in a bad business deal with a partner and I lost about $400,000, out of the blue. I had a wife and three kids that I'm responsible for, and this guy couldn't have cared less. So what was I going to do? Well, I'll tell you. I got a job at FedEx. I'm not trying to pat myself on the back, I'm just telling you how I used what I've been through. I got a job at FedEx and I moved boxes from three o'clock in the morning until seven o'clock in the morning. Then I went to my permanent job as a sub at a high school. I used to have to change my clothes at the Stop N Shop, in the bathroom, so I'd look respectable going into the school. Then, if I could find a tennis court in the afternoon, I'd teach tennis. So, I'm in the third set here. My back is up against the wall. What am I going to do? I'm going to fight.

One of the greatest compliments I ever received came from a best friend of mine. This guy was a quarterback in the NFL. He lived in California and we'd talk often. He said to me one time, "You know, if we weren't good friends and you didn't tell me all the stuff going down in your life, I'd never know you had any problems." I want my players to play like that. I want them to say, "I'm not going to yell, I'm not going to moan. I'm going to say, 'Let's go'." I want them to put their head down and go forward. As I said to my friend, "What options do I have? I could be a miserable bastard or I could suck it up and say, all right, this is what I'm stuck with and I'm going to make the most out of it."

> **"I want my players to play like that. I want them to say, "I'm not going to yell, I'm not going to moan. I'm going to say, 'Let's go'."**

They still say this joke about me at FedEx because I used to walk in every morning and say, "All right, whoever makes the best copy of the Empire State Building with their boxes, I'll give them twenty dollars." They were like, "Get that guy out of here!" *[Laughs]*

I'm sorry, say that again. What was that?

At FedEx, you have to stack the boxes on different lines. For the first couple of days, I said to the guys around me that whoever made the best replica, with their boxes, of the Empire

State Building, I'd give them twenty dollars. You're not supposed to do stuff like that. The boxes have to go in a certain order. But my thought was that I was going in there and I was going to have a good time. I'm just not going to let this beat me. I'm divorced. I have three kids that live two and half hours away from me that I'm very involved with. However, I ended up on my feet. I'm the happiest SOB on the planet for the most part. Tennis deserves a lot of credit, because I've played a lot of hard matches and I was beaten senseless around the head and neck many times. But you learn to keep your head up.

The other thing about tennis is that you can learn a lot about people. I think it's the same with golf. You invite people to play and develop relationships. I used to do this with sales reps all the time, when they came to the club. If you take someone out on the golf course or the tennis court, you can tell a lot about them. If their serve and volley are full on and they're charging the net all the time, that guy is going to go to bat for you. He's going to be aggressive and a tough fighter on your behalf or against you—one of the two.

On the other hand, if somebody hangs around at the base line and just hits the ball back and forth, that guy might not go to bat for you if you get into a tough situation. He's not a fighter. So there's a lot of correlation between how people are and how they play tennis.

I remember my first lesson in mental toughness came when I was ten years old. I was playing a good friend of mine and she was winning 5 games to 2. During the changeover she told me, it doesn't matter what the score is, you still have to believe you can win and sure enough I ended up winning the

set. What do you train your students to think about during those moments when they're behind and the match is slipping away?

It depends on the situation. If they are behind because of a mechanical issue, than I would tell them to slow things down, figure out what is going wrong and do their best to correct the problem. Once that issue is fixed, I would tell them what I would tell any of my players that are down and the match is slipping away; play free, don't worry about the score, and lay it all out but with controlled aggression. Do your best to take it one point at a time and put in your best effort in each of those points! If you are giving your best effort with a laser focus on just being the best "you" out there, than who knows what the outcome will be!

This is the last question... Please tell me who some of your role models are, either in tennis or outside of tennis.

In tennis, aside from Ivan Lendl, probably Rafael Nadal would be one of my role models. I have to say—and this is a little sappy—but I have to say, outside of tennis, my role model is my dad. I worship the ground that man walks on. My father and mother are still alive. My dad is a great father—a very understanding, caring human being. He can get tough when he needs to be tough, but he never goes into a big fit. I can give you an example of when I did what he would have done. My oldest son at the time was in fifth grade. I was visiting him, and he said, "I have a social studies test tomorrow." I said, "What's the test on?" He said, "Oh, I don't know." "You don't know?" I said. "No," he replied. "The teacher goes over everything before class, before the test." I've gone through school and I know you have to study, but, in fifth grade, I figure the ship's not going to sink here. So he goes to school and does his thing. I went back to see him on a Tuesday after the Thursday he told me about the test. I asked him, "How'd you do on your test?" "Not too good," he said. "What did you get?" I asked. "I got a D," he said. I said, "Okay, now it's my turn. You watch your father play matches and exhibitions and stuff. What do I do before I go play?" He says, "You're a crazy man. You change all the grips on the rackets, you put them all in the bags, you put extra socks in the bag, and extra shoes and shirts. You've got a towel to shower with and clean clothes for after your match." I said, "What's that called?" He said, "Getting ready." So I said, "We're going to change that word. It's going to be called preparation." Then I said, "How much preparation did you do before your test?" That's how my dad treated me. I've got to tell you, I really appreciate that type of education because it wasn't like, "Okay, you jerk, you got a D." It was, "Hey, you could do better, and here's how you can do better." So, my dad is a great role model. He messed up plenty too, believe me, but he was a good dad.

Jeff Wilson:

CEO and Co-Owner of the MWTennis Academy at the Family Circle Tennis Center

Coached Six Top 100 Women's Professional Tennis Players

Jeff Wilson

*CEO and Co-Owner of the MWTennis Academy at the Family
Circle Tennis Center, Coached Six Top 100 Women's
Professional Tennis Players*

What pre-match rituals do you recommend to get your players ready for a game?

I think pre-match rituals are incredibly important for a variety of reasons. One of the reasons is that people like consistency. People like to know what to expect. In order to compete at a high level, it's necessary to establish clarity and a sense of calm. This is an interesting process, because in junior tennis, everyone gets overexcited. In college tennis, they get extremely excited too. However, in pro tennis, players look like they're moving in slow motion. They take a lot of time and try to be extremely analytical.

A pre-match ritual is really an individual experience. It's very important to figure out what you, as a coach, like, or what your players like. Once you find a recipe that puts you in the right frame of mind—which is really the whole point—you stay with it. Whether you're in Tokyo or San Francisco or Miami or wherever you happen to be, you need to figure out how much time you need before a match so that you're not rushed. Tennis players hate to be rushed.

Of course, each person is different, so each person needs to figure out if they like to listen to music before a match or they prefer to be alone with their thoughts. There are some people who never like to be alone, so you take that into consideration.

It's different for every player. A good coach is going to figure out what each player's needs are and then try to put together a little pre-match ritual especially for them.

Good players must be really invested in being physically and mentally prepared. During the 10 or 15 minutes before the match, they want to be in a place of complete calm where they can focus all their energies and thoughts on the match. For example, with Irina, we spend time just sitting and talking, which we call "porch time." At a WTA tournament in College Park, there were these nice Adirondack chairs sitting on the porch overlooking the facility. That's where we found ourselves every day, sitting and talking. Pretty soon, she was in the semifinals of the main draw. So, when we sit and talk now, we call it "porch time." During this pre-match ritual, we talk but we really don't talk a lot about tennis. We talk about other things—people, places, different meals, and different experiences. We tell jokes. If you've done your work in terms of preparation, time, tactics, and devising a game plan, then you can relax and slow it down.

A lot of people listen to music and stretch. Some people are highly agitated and need to have somebody talk and joke around with them. Some people need to be motivated, and you've got to get them pumped and fired up. Everyone is different, so each person needs to find the pre-match ritual that works for them.

Say it's match point and championship point. How does a player keep themselves calm and focused in that situation?

We deal with this kind of situation before the match. It's one thing to sit and talk about how to do it. It's quite another thing to experience it! Generally, people fail before they succeed in big moments that are very significant to them. It's important to stay in the moment. That's so easy to say, but the importance of staying locked into your routines, locked into your rituals, and getting into a certain frame of thought can't be overstated. As much as coaches would like to say to players, "In every play and with every point, always keep the same routine," that's just not possible. The worse thing you can do is to think about "What if?. If I do this, this is going to happen, or if I do this, this will happen." You have to go through the different stages and levels of play and work on those things—closing out a match, playing to win here, or recognizing a big point as an opportunity and trying to take that opportunity. This strategy is very different from what goes on in junior tennis, where they're sitting back and hoping the other player misses.

The first key is recognizing that there's an opportunity point coming and it doesn't matter whether it's a match point or a game point or a set point or a championship point. The second thing is recognizing that opportunity. You've got to put yourself in the frame of mind to be playing appropriately, based on the situation. The common criticism that you'll hear from pros is, "I got ahead of myself" or "I started thinking 'what if?'."

Irina played Francesca Schiavone a while back on red clay. At that time, Schiavone was the defending French Open Champ. This was the week before Roland Garros. We were in Brussels, and Irina was up 4-2, 40-30. She was serving and she started thinking about who she was playing. Sure enough, she had a double fault as a result of her tight nerves. Schiavone breaks her, and the next thing you know it's 4-all. A veteran will go up 5-3 because she recognizes, "Hey I've got a chance; I'm going to take it." The rookie says, "Oh gosh, am I really good enough to beat Schiavone on clay?" We still talk about that, and at the time it seemed like a very negative experience. However, if you use it properly, you draw from that experience as you move forward and you don't make the same mistake again.

A big part of being a top-level player is confidence in oneself. How does a player gain that inner confidence to get to the top?

Winning! Let's say, for example, you're ranked 45 in the world and you're playing somebody in the top 10. The person in the top 10 walks out with confidence. The person ranked at 45 has less confidence. Basically, you want to believe you can beat anybody at any time because there really isn't that much difference between the two of you.

So, how do you increase your inner confidence level?

Here's an example: Irina was ranked 85 in the world at the US Open 2011. She was playing in the second round in Arthur Ashe stadium against the number 14 in the world, Dominika Cibulkova. On paper, Cibulkova should have won every time. However, we had a good game plan, and early in the match, during the first two games, the plan worked. It drew the error that we thought it would probably draw. That creates a shot of confidence: "Okay, we're prepared. Okay, the game plan is accurate." Then you just build the self-belief as the course of the match goes on. You have to invest in the proper tactics, be analytical, and not be too worked up when your opponent hits good shots. You have to expect them to hit good shots. That's why they are where they are. When you get your opportunity, you have to recognize it and you have to make a play.

We talk a lot in tennis, just like in football or basketball, because we have to set plays. If I'm going to hit it here, then I'm going to try to elicit this response from my opponent. If we're good at scouting, we know what they like or don't like and we give them what they don't like. We're prepared, just like a quarterback is. A quarterback comes to the line and reads the defense. In basketball, a point guard brings a ball down the court and notices how the defense is set. If you're good at it—as the top 100 in the world are, and there are no flukes—then you know what to do. You take the time to think about tactics and analysis, and you use that information instead of succumbing to doubt. You develop confidence through good preparation and good execution of your plan. Even if you don't get the result you want, if it's close, you can walk away and say, "I had opportunities there, had I just done this or this or this." So, with proper preparation and execution, the confidence grows and you begin to think, "I can play with them." If you get the win, the confidence goes over the top. If you beat a couple people, then you feel like you belong. It's not a fluke.

If you're prepared for what you think will happen using plan A and plan B, and you're making consistent adjustments that are appropriate, then it simply comes down to execution of those shots. If you're able to execute and you do it on purpose, then the confidence goes through the roof and you can start to build a career out of that. At the same time, you can be exposed. If you're not prepared, you don't know what's **"That's why coaches or analysts say, "This kid is going to be good," because they see the positive things within their game and notice the player isn't worried about who's on the other side of the net. "** happening in the match, or you aren't really clear on what adjustments your opponent made, that becomes apparent. But the good news is that there's room to develop. That's why coaches or analysts say, "This kid is going to be good," because they see the positive things within their game and notice the player isn't worried about who's on the other side of the net. Frankly once you're out on tour for a while, you find yourself in the same locker room with the same people every single week. It's always the same, and the wow-factor or the, "Oh my gosh, it's Federer" sort of wears off. Well, actually, with Federer, it's different. People still get wild about him. But overall, self-belief and confidence comes from executing a plan on a consistent basis. Generally, that leads to a win. Whether it's winning a game, a set, a match, or winning a tournament, there are so many different levels of depth. When you're playing at the tour level, any time you win, you gain. If you can win on purpose by executing your plan, and you're accurate in your assessments, then there's a huge gain.

What's the most important thing to think about during a changeover?

During the changeover, you're analyzing information. That's all you're doing, if you're good. You're analyzing information. If something is working and it's extremely simple, the hard part is staying disciplined enough to stay with the simple plan and not to get distracted or move away from it. Your self-talk is about analyzing what's going on out there, because now you're resting your body, you're cooling off, and you're giving yourself an opportunity to say, "Okay, what do I want to do in this two-game segment? What am I looking for my opponent to do? Are they going to make any adjustments? Do I need to make any adjustments?" The changeover time goes really, really fast. In the WTA, coaches are allowed to come out once a set at tour events and coach during the changeover. In college, you're able to do it every point; you can give the player a verbal interaction every point at the college level. At the pro level, if the player is good, they're thinking about information and figuring out what they want to come out doing or not doing. It's as simple as that.

Butterflies and nerves have the ability to be a positive force for success if channeled correctly. How do you tell your players to channel their butterflies in the correct way?

Yeah, I love that. As a coach, you love that. As a player, I loved it. It means there's a sense of urgency. This is the moment! I tell them, "Hit the crap out of the ball for the first two or three shots of the warm-up." Usually, by the end of the first three points in the pro level, you're fine. You're okay because you've been there before and you draw on past experiences. As a coach, you try to give your players analogies such as, "This will be just like that was" or "This match will play out like that one did" or "Once you play on Arthur Ashe, nothing else is a big deal." Arthur Ashe is the biggest stage and people are commentating. You look up and McEnroe is there. You know what they're saying because you grew up watching it on TV. So, once you have that experience, it's good to have the nerves, because it means the adrenaline is going. That means the energy is there and you know the focus is going to kick in. When a kid isn't worried or a pro isn't worried, that's when I get worried, to be honest. If you think Nadal is never nervous or Federer isnt nervous, you're mistaken. Everybody who goes out there either has a lot to lose or a lot to gain. There's always an angle that's playing in someone's head.

However, if you hang onto those nerves for more than a minute or two, that's a problem. If I sense a player is letting his nerves get the best of him, I make a comment from the coach's box such as, "Let's go!" But again, you prepare for it, and that's the importance of the pre-match ritual, the "porch time." That preparation is critical for success at the high level. Deal with the nerves by hitting the ball or through breathing or by just hitting through your nerves. That's the best way to do it.

What's your opinion of players who don't think they have what it takes to be a professional player, even though it's their life's dream?

If they don't think they have it, they don't. Period! Pro tennis at the high level has nothing to do with forehands, backhands, and serves. It has nothing to do with that. It has to do with self-belief, conviction, confidence, and physical and mental effort. If you have to convince somebody that they're good enough, then they're not good enough. It has to come from them. If you asked me to point out a commonality at the high level, it's that. It's the self-belief.

If someone thinks they're not good enough to be a pro, I'd tell them, "Okay, you're not good enough and you should do something else. Don't go this way." That's probably harsh, but it will save everyone a lot of time and money. On the flip side, if they think they're good enough and they don't have the tools, a good coach can help them get those tools. Whether they end up mastering those tools is a different issue. However, even if you're selling someone on confidence at the pro level on a consistent basis, it's not going to work out if they don't believe in themselves.

What's the trick to having a healthy tennis attitude on a consistent basis?

Healthy tennis attitude... It's a game that's fun to play, right? I think a lot of pros lose sight of that and play it as a job, and you can see that in their game. I think a lot of juniors lose sight of it also. Most juniors lose sight of how fun it is and treat it as work, so the emotion you see is generally negative or overly dramatic. Having a sense of the intrinsic fun of playing or competing and testing yourself is critical for longevity in our sport.

It's one thing if you don't enjoy doing nine million sprints. I don't know if anybody enjoys that piece of it, but it's a necessity at the pro level. If you're out there hitting balls and you don't find it fun, that's a problem. It's a game. Even though there's a lot of business attached to it when you get to the higher level, it's still a game. I think a lot of people who struggle—I'm not going to mention names, but I can think of several friends of mine who are struggling on the women's tour right now—have simply lost the sense of how much fun tennis is and how lucky they are to be playing this game for a living. You've got to have a good perspective on what it's all about. But again, when you go to junior tennis tournaments, you see the parents living vicariously through their kids. Fifty percent of the parents out there want it more than the kid does, and it gets really dicey. In college, it gets less and less dicey, but in the pros, when it stops being fun, you need to take some time away. This is a fundamental of long-term success in anything: If you hate your job, you're going to quit your job. You're going to find a reason to fail. If you love it, then you're going to find a reason to flourish and enjoy it.

How do you recommend young players keep a balanced life but still have the appropriate emphasis on tennis?

I think the appropriate emphasis is an individual thing. Some people have more athletic talent than others and some people have more financial resources than others, which plays a big factor. However, hard work and perseverance is going to overcome talent every time in the long run. My own son is eleven and I don't have him playing that many tournaments. You can't gain a lot as an eleven-year-old, globally, but you can lose a lot. I think as kids get older, as long as they have the proper skills, tools, and a sense of how to play the game, they're going to develop into mature people and mature bodies. Everything will be different when they're eighteen. What you do when you're ten, eleven, or twelve really doesn't mean a thing, in my opinion. Play other sports, do other things, and also play tennis. At some point, if your focus starts to narrow and your goals start to become more and more specific, then you need to begin to drop other things.

The biggest mistake I see out there is kids are being home-schooled at age nine or ten and are isolating themselves on the tennis court. I see the results of this at the pro level. The amount of people at the pro level who have nice social skills and the ability to interact on an intelligent basis with other people is very small, and it's purely because of the lifestyle they've lived for the previous ten years. This is usually because of the parents. The parents are driving most of this stuff. Junior tennis has a really aggressive and negative atmosphere in the United States. Yes, there are exceptions, but that's pretty much the standard rule. A lot of kids aren't out there to have fun. They're out there to win at all costs. As a result, you get bad line calls, you get parents cheating, you get dominating parents, you get a lot of verbal interaction during matches. I watch this as a coach and as a parent and I don't want that for my players or for my kids.

The culture we have at my academy is positive. The focus is on the team and on manners, which includes eye contact, handshakes, and those kinds of life skills. The tennis is very, very easy; it just takes a long time. It's easy to get better at forehands and backhands, but I think variety is important and I think continuing to focus on building life skills and putting kids and people in different situations is vital.

Too often I see pros not taking advantage of a city that they're in, even when it's a really cool city, because they're in a tournament. They won't even go out to dinner. They're just there to work and to win an extra $1000. This is great, but you're really not going to remember a second match when you're 65 years old. However, you're probably going to remember seeing Salzburg for a night. I think people need to enjoy what tennis gives them on a more consistent basis because it's such a great sport and a great game and a great global experience. Parents are wrecking it at the junior level because of the lifestyle decisions that are being forced on these kids. There are no nine-year-olds saying, "I want to be home schooled." Every nine-year-old says, "Yeah, of course, I don't want to get up at six and come home at four every day. Give me another option and I'm going to be like, yes, this is the best thing in the world." Then that same kid at thirteen can't carry on a conversation and we wonder why.

What sort of goal-setting practices do you use with your players?

For pros and, for example, Irina, there are process goals and outcome goals. The outcome goals are stated objectives, and we set process goals to try to achieve the outcomes goals. So, for Irina, she had her goals for 2012 and we set our competitive schedule in quarters. We do three months at a time. We set smaller outcome goals within the quarters and set process goals to try to achieve those outcomes. They could be anything for anybody. In junior tennis or college tennis, for example, a goal could be, "I want to have a more effective kick serve," In order to achieve that, I'm going to hit 60 kick serves a day, five days a week for five weeks. That gives me 300 kick serves a week or 1500 serves at the end of five weeks. At the end of five weeks, I should have a much better kick serve, right? That's how we look at development goals.

However, most parents talk about rankings and talk about points. When I ask kids to list strengths, weaknesses, and goals, rarely do they reply, "I want to accrue this many points" or "I want to get a ranking of this." They always say, "I want to get better. I want to keep having fun."

In addition, I look at grade-point average for juniors; that's a great goal. I look at attendance records for practice, which is also a great goal. I look at tournament matches and number of matches played in a year, which are also good. And through those types of goals, generally you're building good people, you're building good students, and you're building a good tennis player. It's a tough sell on the parents, because they want the kids to win, win, win, win, now, now, now because parents get treated differently at tournaments when their kids are at the top. It's like a celebrity status kind of deal. But, like I said, it's different at every level because different stages of development necessitate different goals. Process goals and outcomes goals are extremely individual to each player.

If you're good at it, you set appropriate and reachable goals but, most importantly, attainable goals. Through this goal-setting, you see who wants to be good and who doesn't. As a coach, all you do is facilitate those goals. If Johnny comes to me with six goals, I'll tell him what he's going to need to do to achieve them and we do the work together. But, in America, the kid that sets goals and follows through is one in a thousand. One in a thousand. Everybody talks about getting a scholarship, but you don't just sign up for a college scholarship. You earn it through hard work and dedication over several years.

How do players push themselves, or how does a coach push their players when they don't feel like training?

That's a good question. As a coach, you have to know

your people. There were so many days, as a player, that I didn't feel like training. In college, you find a reason to not go or you find a reason to give a sub-par effort. In the pros, if you're not practicing, then you're not going to make any money. You have to be intrinsically self-motivated to work at it, because it's your job. However, most people don't see it that way. Most people don't see it as a job that requires them to be self-motivated.

Because I run my own academy, the buck stops with me and honestly, some days it's tougher to be motivated than others but then we'll have a rain day or two and I'll get refreshed and feel energized again. Generally, if you're a good coach, you look at your personnel and, if it's an individual setting, you do something different to get the player interested. You make the practice fun, you give them a challenge, you figure out what makes each player tick, and you put them in situations to be challenged. Because there are good relationships in place with the other players and coaches, the player can enjoy it and have fun with it. You just have to know each person. As a culture and as a program, the kids will govern the other kids. Most of the time, a kid will get motivated once they get going. The hard part is getting there and getting going. You just have to figure out each person and what they're all about and put them in positions to challenge themselves. Sometimes we play games because it's fun. Sometimes we play matches. Sometimes we slice only. Sometimes we just mix things up and try to work on something that needs working on without making it feel like work. You can make it enjoyable, by mixing in a game that's fun.

With most people, if they're competitive, there's a paradigm shift that happens in their head once you start keeping score. They'll go out and compete until all of a sudden, they're through it. That's very rewarding as a coach, and those are some of your best days, when you manage that.

Who do you think are the most mentally tough male and female professional players out there right now?

Nadal, by a mile. I mean, by a mile, an absolute mile. Djokovic is obviously showing signs. But with Nadal, year in and year out for six years, every match is just…every practice session is just incredible. He motivates me, and I'm pretty good at what I do. He helps make me better, and I don't even know him.

On the women's side, I think… It's a lot tougher question, isn't it? It's a lot more wide open. Everybody on the women's tour seems to have a gift, but everybody seems to have a breaking point. Right now, at this moment, I'd say Azarenka, based on 2012. She lost one set in three tournaments in 2012. I think of Kim Clijsters, leaving the game and then coming back as a mother and winning a couple slams after that. That shows some mental toughness, because of the off-the-court life changes.

How have the skills you've gained from the tennis court translated to your after-tennis life? What do you hope young players take from their tennis experience?

First and foremost, if you've finished a successful professional career, the number of relationships you have around the world is a significant thing. Your life skills, your ability to travel, your perspective on how different cultures do things is a very big benefit. The ability to be independent on the road on a consistent basis and to navigate the globe is important. I think that if you're a good person, through your travels and your experiences you'll have met a lot of people and you can give back and realize how much it takes every week and every tour stop, whether it's a minor league $25,000 tournament or a grand slam. You realize and appreciate that each event is one of the highlights of that town's year. Someone who's aware of all that and someone who looks at all the different kids that are impacted by what they see these pros doing will realize they have a great opportunity to give back through the game of tennis. To make a life out of it is such a unique opportunity and should be appreciated.

Just because you stop playing in your mid-30s doesn't mean you're done. What you do afterwards is really critical and even more important than what you did as a player. Tennis provides you with a lifestyle in which you're able to impact kids' lives and people's lives around the world. You can do this through a long career in the game or through a charitable foundation or through broadcasting, coaching, or whatever. You can mostly do things on your terms instead of in a corporate culture. A lot of people would like to do this, but they're too scared.

Tennis is just a fun way to live your life. That's what it's been for me. I'm 41 and I've got a wife and three kids. Tennis has taken me to over 65 countries so far, and I've been lucky enough to coach in all the Grand Slams, win NCAA titles, win ACC Championships at Duke and Georgia Tech, and win national titles at the junior level.

Some of my most rewarding moments have happened at the lowest level of the game, where a kid wins a match for the first time ever at a 10-and-under or 12-and-under event. Those accomplishments are just as memorable to me as big tournament wins with well-known players. The joy you get from giving to people through our sport is immeasurable. That's what I would hope to convey to any of the kids or adults that I work with— how lucky they are to be playing a game like this and how much they can use this vehicle to change people's lives. So, that's my answer!

ACKNOWLEDGEMENTS

Since the inception of this project over two years ago, thank G-d, there have been many people that have helped bring this book to completion and without them, this book would not have been possible. Most importantly, I would like to thank my good friend Patricia Jensen who is always setting the bar higher and higher for generosity and friendship. This book would not have been completed with out her efforts and I greatly appreciate it. In addition, I would like to thank my family, for always showing support, interest and advice whenever I needed it. To the first person I brought on board to help me, Yehudit Finkel, who not only spent countless hours transcribing the interviews, but also continued to push me to get it done, up until the very end. My graphic designer Karen Pezzuti, who has been on board since the beginning and never disappoints in the creativity she brings to each project. I would also like to thank Jane Steinmetz of Splendid Work, LLC for her advice and encouragement since the beginning. And last but certainly not least I would like to thank all the coaches who generously gave their time and insight to make this book what it is: Michael Center, Ellis Ferreira, Philip Farmer, Chuck Kriese, Luke Jensen, Bruce Levine and Jeff Wilson. Thank you very much to all of you; I hope that you are all proud of the result.

26745681R00095

Printed in Great Britain
by Amazon